SIR JOHN BLACK'S BENTLEY MARK VI

B342NZ

DROPHEAD FOURSOME COUPE

History, Restoration and Significance

By Leon Garoyan, Ph.D.
Former member: RROC, RREC, BDC

Classic Car Club of
America
Master Judge #86

ISBN: 978-1-952337-56-7

Library of Congress Control Number: 2021924197

Preface

The restoration of this Bentley began shortly after I acquired the car in October, 2010. The first constructive efforts were to determine what the project's activities should be; that is, we start such a project with a format called "planning". In past restorations I have used an engineer's process referred to as a Pert Network, that is a planning tool of obtaining materials or parts, and interrelations of what activities must be completed before other activities can be started and time estimates required of each account. This planning tool was an outgrowth during WW 2 by allied engineers.

The fact the car is a true, rare, one-off Bentley convertible, produced by Mulliners of Birmingham, a coachbuilder that began making carriages in 1792 is very rare. For example, the terms and the meaning may have changed over time between models. Having been designed by Stuart Peck, who earned his credentials by assisting very prominent coachbuilders but who had not designed an entire car from stem to stern is significant. Furthermore, as a young designer who was inspired by prominent designers of French reputation a generation earlier, he was able to combine French cultural style designs to traditional English engineering is a testament to his brilliance. Craftsmen in the same industry in different countries may function differently. With the story of Sir John, the car became dynamically spectacular. I know of no other car with these credentials.

Capping acknowledgement at this point, not earlier, are my respects for a person of knowledge and experience whom I have known for many years and projects. He is Chris Clarke, a car enthusiast of distinction, true to his fellowman, and just as enthusiastically a good friend, who guided me in many facets of bringing this car to where it is now. If you do not yet know Chris, I hope you will have the opportunity soon. He is an educator, a student of car technology and a helpful friend.

I was excited to have had the privilege to own this car and to bring together a group of craftsmen who have pride in their work. In that sense the attitude of an artist occasionally prevailed among them. As you look over the finished Bentley photos of the "artists pride", I hope you will see pride of accomplishment of five or more skilled craftsmen in the workmanship of the restoration of this car.

Finally, I developed much pride in being able to be a part of the restoration of the original grandeur to the original work of Sir John Black, and the pride of its designer Stuart Peck, and others responsible for its creation and care. I developed tremendous respect and admiration for Sir John; I hope in time his lifetime accomplishments for England, his people, wartime service, and for those present-day sports car enthusiasts will enjoy his contributions to sports car motoring. In my opinion Sir John is long overdue such respect.

Leon Garoyan, Ph.D.

Acknowledgements

I have had the privilege of owning over 115 cars during my lifetime of 96 years, and most have given me great satisfaction. I have owned some of these cars for many years. The longest was the 1955 Mercedes 300 S roadster, which I owned for 47 years before it received a professional cosmetic restoration. Then a 1930 Rolls-Royce Hooper P II All-weather touring sedan (143GN) owned for 43 years, that won the RROC Hooper Award. Also, a 1930 Pierce-Arrow dual cowl phaeton for 28 years (which won the Most Elegant Open Car Award in 1988 at the Pebble Beach Concourse d'Elegance .) These were followed by a 1934 Pierce-Arrow model 1240 convertible coupe, a 1937 Pierce Arrow model 1701, and with my son, Leon III, a 1970 Mercedes Benz 300 SL, all being first class winners in national competition. In each instance, these cars were professionally restored, with my amateur involvement.

That has been true with my ownership and restoration of Sir John's 1952 Model VI Bentley, a rare one-off convertible of significant heritage. Sir John was awarded his Knighthood from King George VI for his service to his beloved England in 1943. He served his professional career as managing Director of Standard Motor Car Company for about 28 years. To my knowledge this is the only complete book about this one-off car that honors Sir John Black.

Unlike most of my car restorations, this car has experienced many firsts for me, notably the many friends I have come to know and worked with internationally. To these friends, I acknowledge uncommon thanks. There are no "first and seconds" in naming these gentle people, but certainly, becoming a friend with Nick Black, the surviving son of Sir John has touched me immensely. Nick has shared many confidences and other information with me, and guided me through his years of information as an author of an informative book titled Triumph and Tragedy, about his father's career as an industrialist, his public service to his country, and as a parent who suffered both joy and sorrow. I became somewhat acquainted with Sir John as a result of my acquaintance with Nick; I fear I learned but the surface about this amazing leader and businessman, whom I hope someday will be better known within his own country for his accomplishments worthy of being a legend.

Also, from England's auto industry and an active member of RREC is Tony J. Jenkin, former registrar of the MD VI & Silver Wraith Register. Had we lived in closer proximity, I believe Tony and I would be personal friends, and not just because we like the same model Bentley. Tony James, an icon within the RREC provided information that guided me when I could have taken a wrong turn. Then, there is Peter Weston, who supplied uncanny knowledge and sources of hardware for a one-off car adorned with unusual handles, cranks, and door and trunk locks. Then along came Graham Robinson, a native of England at the time living in Brazil, who responded to my request for information on

English owners of this car after Sir John's sale after only 14 months of ownership. With uncanny sleuthing Graham came up with vast information about the prior owners, and also several of their descendants.

For technical information, Norman Geeson, a professional with the highest levels of information on mechanics of these cars was most helpful. Norman serves as a technical consultant to the RROC as well as a writer of distinction. Norman researched and provided technical drawings from RREC files. Then when I wanted to learn about the coachbuilder (Mulliners of Birmingham) I was referred to W.O. Morrison, honorary archivist for the W.O. Bentley Foundation. We exchanged correspondence rather faithfully over several years.

Moving along, Richard Treacy, of Australia and for years a resident of Switzerland until his return in 2012, became my "business partner" as he helped me find a machinist in Australia with an interest and technical capabilities to machine the special not available pins and bushings for the rear shackles of the Mark VI. I also mention Gerard Leclerc, friend and founding President of Section Romande, of RREC in Geneve, for his eager support.

Domestically, the list of people who provided substantial assistance is lengthy, and doing so is fraught with danger since I may overlook some. To not make that mistake within my household, my spouse Nina is mentioned first, for untold help in many ways. She has been a great one to lean on, as always. Richard Howitt, a long-time friend and colleague always comes through at timely occasions when he senses I need help. Then, other friends from the Northern California Chapter of RROC include John Carey, Ivan Gallo, and Jim Weager, who each spent days at a time working as a "guest worker". From Henderson, Nevada, Greg Wood, a friend by his own right and son of my most valuable mentor, the late Professor Burton Wood, both have entrenched themselves in my soul. Then, Roy Dryer, internationally known artist (of classic cars and wood boats) always helps in paint and color designs that result in unearned compliments for me.

Steven Galdrige, who rebuilt my P II Rolls engine in about 1983 has remained as my main mechanical genius for these and other cars. When I ran into the need for mechanical and electrical expertise with B342NZ, I called on Steven again.

Finally, Mark Milton, who was a neighbor at age 13 when he started to teach me how to get myself out of mechanical problems while I worked on my collector cars has been extremely helpful, again. Or, I should say, "still". I wish I had adopted him years ago, since we have remained close family friends for 44 years.

Special Recognition to my Dear Friends, The Howitts

It isn't how long I've known Richard and Jeri Howitt over the years, it's how we have supported each other as though by anticipation.

My friendship with Richard and his mother living in England date back over 55 years. His mother lived near Windsor and kept several of my cars on their farm in storage, and overlooked at maintaining them from year to year for me.

I looked after her vineyard when I stayed with them on the farm.

In California, Richard and Jeri helped move my cars, after my first classic cars back in 1970. As I bought other cars, they offered their care, as though they anticipated the car's needs.

Richard and Jeri have been life friends these many years, wherever I had a car needing care, just as would relatives. We have mutually owned lovely cars, and admire them blessedly. Few people would have such friendship. I love them tremendously.

I thank also those professionals who helped reduce my bank reserves during the 5 years of this restoration, and whose skills show what it took to make the car what it is today. Included are Tom Boutos (deceased), Jeff Norene, Steven Bennett, and Rich Biner.

Lee Garoyan

CHAPTER 1

Finding and Preserving Sir John Black's Bentley

Sir John Black, a gentleman with historic attachments to the British car industry commissioned a 1952 one-off Bentley four-passenger convertible coupe in 1950 that nearly became lost in a California garage. Sixty years later, the car became available and was acquired for restoration by a collector. Sir John also made significant contributions in two World Wars, yet he is virtually unknown despite his automotive and wartime contributions. There's more to the story than this introduction implies.

Now the rest of the story

When I purchased this one-off convertible foursome coupe in 2010, I had little knowledge of how it came to be commissioned, by whom, and for what purpose. As we became involved with planning to "fix" this nice car, we wondered about its history. I discovered Sir John's son, Nick, who had just written *Triumph & Tragedy*, a book about his father. Getting a copy of that book triggered an awareness of the remarkable story that brought car and Sir John into a perspective both needed.

A bit about Sir John (more comes later)

Sir John Black had served important military roles during two World Wars for his native England. After WW 2 he returned full time to his post as managing director of Standard Motor Cars, Ltd. In that capacity Sir John turned his attention to the future of the British motor industry. He commissioned and assisted in the design of a Bentley Mark VI convertible foursome. He had previously owned several Bentley cars, though he had no corporate ties with Rolls-Bentley. He owned this rare Bentley for only 13 months after its delivery. The lovely designed car had served its purpose. Ten years later, with two intervening owners, it was purchased by a new owner in California.

Sir John is arguably one of three or four of the most influential industrialists responsible for the development and success of the British motor industry, yet he is the least acclaimed and least recalled. His story in the motor industry of England began in joint management of the Hillman Motor Company in 1921, and he shifted to the management group of Standard Motor Company Ltd. in 1929 and ended in 1954. Between these years he was a dominant figure with manufacturers of family-oriented cars, some of which became developers of a sports car industry. In fact, Standard Motors, the company he now managed, supplied engines, gearboxes and other engineered parts to many small car manufacturers that made it possible for them to exist to build "sports cars".

In addition, his remarkable roles in two World Wars have been masked by more flamboyant personalities and the passage of time. More about this interesting industrialist in this context follows in a later section.

Sir John is responsible for developing a 1952 Mark VI convertible coupe, B342NZ, that my staff has preserved to factory-new condition.

A bit about a 1952 Bentley Mark VI

After disappearing from view and memories for 38 years in dry storage in northern California, B342NZ, the 1952 Mark VI four-passenger convertible was offered for sale by the widow of its last owner. With upwards of 30 collectors and restorers giving serious consideration, the car was purchased by Leon Garoyan. His crew immediately began to plan its restoration, and after 4 years of effort by a team of five subcontractor-specialists in auto restoration, B342NZ, neared the time to be unveiled to the public; a car that began as a restoration project thus ended as a preservation of the unique designs and constructions by its final craftsmen.

In the fall months of 2014 we expected B342NZ would be ready for her first showing, largely to collectors and the select group who are experienced with successful introductions of unique cars.

B342NZ was accepted for competition at the world-wide prestigious 2014 Pebble Beach Concours d'Elegance, in the class of "Post-war Sports and GT" cars.

What constitutes a collector's item?

Consider the usual variables that make a car a highly prized and valued item, including one or more of these characteristics:

- a one-off example with attractive design;
- famous former or original owner;
- behemoth, monstrously big, fast driver;
- racing or record speed history;
- prototype for a succeeding line of cars that created vigor in car sales or manufacturing; or
- special design and attractiveness that give substantial character to an amazing car.

In what follows, it's owner, Leon Garoyan, describes the series of decisions and activities that make this 1952 Bentley Mark VI an attractive investment.

Description of Mark VI Bentley Cars

The Bentley Mark VI represented the first post-WW 2 development by Rolls-Bentley of a luxury car designed for owner-drivers. Immediate steps toward post-war economic development for the UK included developing an export market for sports cars to create markets and jobs. Prior to the war, Rolls-Bentley built chassis and cowls in their factories but private coachbuilders designed bodies to car buyer's specifications. After WW 2 Rolls-Bentley standardized body design and constructed these in-house.

Building bodies in R-R and Bentley factories helped create jobs, made owner-driver cars easier to maintain because of standardization of body parts, and broadened the market for its cars that gave the factory more control of marketing. The Mark VI was a turning point in this practice, allowing more control for the factory, as was common with other luxury carmakers.

The impact of this practice on British car buyers was favorable. Bernard L. King, lauded historian of Bentley and Rolls-Royce cars comments about the acceptance of the Mark VI by notable people including heads of other car companies:

> "It is astounding how many other vehicle manufacturers opted for Mark VI cars for use of their executives, William Lyons of Jaguar had B357GB, B55FU and B123NZ, Leonard Lord of Austin used B246AK, Archie Frazer-Nash had B9NY John Sangster-owner of Triumph Motorcycles had B494CF and Sir John Black of Standard Co. commissioned another of his companies, Mulliners Ltd. of Birmingham to build a one-off drop head on chassis B342NZ, which eventually replaced a standard steel car B337EW".

> "Numerous individuals from the entertainment and arts industry are also listed by King as owners of these cars; Elton John, Laurence Olivier, Ingrid Bergman, Charlie Chaplin, Diana Dors, George Formby and Donald Peers".
> (Page 30, Bentley Mk. VI, A Complete Classics Publication, England, 2007).

Technical Data

Early production Mark VI cars were fitted with a 4,256 cc engine. Beginning in 1951 with Chassis MEMD a "big bore" engine was used, with a more powerful 4,566 cc engine. This resulted in improvements of speed and performance, a requisite for a sports car (B342NZ was one of the cars fitted by the factory with the "big bore" engine). Rated at top speeds of 105 mph these cars were more than capable of holding their own with other luxury cars on the improved motorways. (Technical data are attached as an appendix).

Features of B342NZ, Sir John Black's Custom Bentley

From 1934 through 1954 Sir John Black served as managing director of Standard Motors, a long established auto company that produced numerous marques of family cars. During WW 2, Sir John guided England to shift auto production resources to the production of airplane engines and fuselages, armored vehicles, and other armaments to meet wartime needs. After WW 2, peace gradually returned to the Nation and a need arose to start the industrial revitalization process towards peacetime needs. Sir John planned for that by attempts with other car manufacturers to develop and increase output of sports cars, an effort that included expanding manufacturing of Triumph, a car company owned by Standard Motors.

In 1939, he and Mulliners of Birmingham, the coachbuilder, had designed and built a razor edge saloon on a SS100 (Jaguar) chassis they intended to make a sportier family saloon. Having also acquired the Triumph Company in 1944, Standard introduced several models of the Triumph sport cars after WW 2. From these heady days of 1950-51, came the idea to commission Mulliners of Birmingham to design and manufacture this Bentley Mark VI drop head coupe for Sir John. This allowed more in-house development and design time for Triumph. As a result, the TR-2 was created in 1952 and the TR-3 introduced in 1955, both successfully competing with other English sports cars for export sales. Some car enthusiasts feel that the B342NZ may have been a prototype design for these TRs.

Unique, distinctive features of B342NZ

Stuart Peck designed this car from stem to stern. Prior to his engagement with Mulliners of Birmingham, Peck had been affiliated with a number of major coachbuilders of the period, including A. F. McNeil of James Young and Gurney Nutting. Peck was impressed with the French school of auto designers, including Henri Chapron and Joseph Figoni. The shape and configuration of the rear wings and rear wheel skirts (spats) of this car reflect a French influence.

- This body was the only Bentley/Rolls built by Mulliners of Birmingham after WW 2. (Mulliners was acquired by Standard Motors in 1958).

- The front wings of B342NZ likely served as a prototype for the design of the TR-2, the successful sports car model that was marketed

4

internationally by Standard Motors following WW 2. Later, similar designs appeared on fenders of coach-built Mark VI's built by competing coachbuilders.

- Unlike many coach built bodies of that post-war era, this body was built of steel rather than aluminum, providing considerably more strength that reduces flexing of a convertible body.

- Only 13 months after its delivery by Mulliners of Birmingham, Sir John sold the car to E. C. Poynter of Surrey, who a year later sold the car to Leslie Onslow, a man of many skills, including racing automobiles. His racing of the Mark VI proves the ability of the 4 ½ liter, six-cylinder engine for agility, speed, and sustainability.

- Some believe after the design of B342NZ had served its purpose as a prototype and encouraged a divided board of SMC to accept some of the designs for the newly planned TR range, Sir John had made his point. The SMC board gave another Bentley to Sir John as a part of his Termination Agreement in 1954. As history indicates, the TR3 became and remains a collectors' sports car worldwide.

Sir John Black (1895-1965) by Cowan Dobson

We cannot confirm that Sir John commissioned the car for personal use during Queen Elizabeth's coronation celebrations in 1953. According to this rumor, Sir John was said to have ties with the Royal Family, perhaps resulting from his WW 2 activities that led to his being Knighted by King George VI. Though an interesting story, we have only found anecdotal information to support this notion.

The car's early life

B342NZ was registered in Sir John's name when delivered in 1952 but spent only 13 months in his possession. There were two owners during the next 10 years when the car remained in England.

E. C. Poynter, from Surrey, was the second registered owner. He kept the car only a short period until 1953 when Leslie Onslow of Bournemouth became the next registered owner. Onslow was an interesting person with varied occupations, including chaperoning ladies to ballroom dancing events and racing motorcars, including B342NZ. He obviously found the car a very good racecar, since he kept it nearly 8 or 9 years before he sold the car to Jack Compton Ltd., a prominent Rolls/Bentley dealer in the U.K. In 1962 C. E. Gelber of Encino, California bought the car from Compton.

Life in California

Mr. Gelber made it a daily driver for about 6 years. In correspondence with a subsequent owner, he thought he had driven the car about 110,000 miles during that time. The next owner was A. Sheratin Atkinson, located in the San Francisco Bay Area, who kept the car for about 5 years.

The anticipation of Dr. Kurt Hammerstrom, its third owner in California must have been tremendous, given that he began a personal restoration of the car in 1973.

Dr. Hammerstrom was a person of multiple interests besides the Bentley. As many individual car restorers have experienced, the tasks of a complete undertaking often exceed the time available and the years of attention needed for a complete restoration. He kept the partly dismantled car in dry storage from 1973 to 2010, when Dr. Leon Garoyan purchased the car from his widow. True to his professional training as a dentist, the car's parts were neatly stored in cartons, and for 38 years dispersed throughout his garage and portions of the dry basement of his house. Later, after Dr. Garoyan's purchase of the car, this orderly compartmentalization enabled him to fairly quickly reassemble the car to determine the missing parts needed to buy.

Almost a barn find-certainly a rare find

Few people other than Dr. Kurt Hammerstrom and his widow, Molly, knew about the existence of the car after 38 years in storage. Molly Hammerstrom contacted Austin Kilburn, a prominent member of the Northern California region of the Rolls-Royce Owners Club, to request guidance in selling the dismantled car. Within a week of calling many RROC members, upwards of 30 individuals had inspected the car.

The restoration process

As with many restorations the extent of work required to bring the car to its desired condition kept changing, for several reasons. Problems of restoring a one-off body hinge around the fact that such bodies are different from all others. Door design and fit differ from another one-off body. Fender design and other panel designs vary because they are unique to a given car. Thus, whenever a repair or replacement is required, it must be hand fabricated, as was the original body. Restoring a one-off car is like starting from original diagrams and drawings. The restorer has to understand the logic of the unique body design and its construction. In this case the following helped us.

- As we proceeded in our cleanup work, we learned a lot of the work that had gone into the design and fabrication of the body by Stuart Peck, its designer, and Mulliners of Birmingham, its builder. Tom Boutos my metal craftsman/fabricator described time after time, "this is a strong body", attesting to the quality of the design and the work of the original craftsmen.

- Based on what we were learning, the historical significance of both B342NZ and Sir John had faded in public awareness. Despite his years of important service to his Country he received limited public exposure except for being Knighted by King George VI in 1943. His retirement came soon after his success in helping to lead the post-war trends with sports car manufacturing that created employment and success for the British car industry.

- As with the work of an acclaimed artist whose final work went out of circulation, Sir John and the Bentley were denied the tributes they would have if the car and the man had remained longer in visibility.

- We perceived this car as the find of a new artist, with a new work of art unbeknownst to the public. We believe it is a new find of significance.

The most significant features of a one-off car are evident in the body design, configuration and design of upholstery and seats, and structural features that give distinction to the ideas of the body designers.

- How body contours help create sleek eye appealing profiles.

- How desirable visual flow patterns can be developed by metal fabrication.

Strength, integrity and stability of the body are overall necessities. These desirable original characteristics are preserved with B342NZ.

One-off cars are obviously rare

According to King, out of a total of 5,208 Mark VI Cars made, 73 were one-off of all body types. Of these, only 20 were drop head coupes. B342NZ is the only Mark VI drop head coupe, and the only Bentley body made by Mulliners of Birmingham (King: Bentley Mark VI tables, pg. 363-377).

There were three coachbuilders in England with the name of "Mulliner", and some confusion exists about each. In this book we are referring to Mulliners of Birmingham, as the coachbuilder for B342NZ. This company was founded in 1897 by Herbert Mulliner, who was related to Arthur and H.J., the other Mulliners. During 1924, Louis Antweiler purchased the company and established close working relations with the Standard Motor Co. In 1958 Antweiler's Mulliner company was acquired by the Standard-Triumph Group.

At times during our restoration we encountered opportunities to use more modern fabrication methods that enhance the lines of the car without altering its originality. We opted to use such methods as appropriate. Sometimes this required creating new panels to replace earlier repairs by others.

We also fitted panels and door assemblies to make sure the fits were properly aligned. For example, the original design made no allowance for quarter window alignment with the top hardware, so adjustment mechanisms were designed to provide future adjustment potentials. The result has been consistent gaps, spacing and fitting of adjoining panels. Still, the final result is a car that reflects its former grandeur with newer construction procedures as could be integrated into the original creation.

Chassis

The chassis was in good repair, with normal usage. After removing the body, the chassis and mechanical gears underwent restoration. All components attached to the frame were removed, cleaned, inspected, repaired as needed, and reattached to the frame. The Bijur central lubrication system was operationally checked, the front suspension received inspection and was rebuilt, brake and brake drum assemblies received like treatment, as did the related brake servo system. Following this cleanup, inspection, and worn parts replaced, the frame was powder-coated and put in final condition.

The engine was dismantled and taken to a machine shop for detailed analysis. The crankshaft was found to be within original clearances, so its surfaces were polished, the original cylinder half liners were extracted and as recommended by the factory, replaced with full cylinder liners, new pistons and rings fitted, and other engine components inspected and replaced as needed. A new vibration damper was installed, dual carburetors sent out for repair and restoration, new ignition wires installed, and in all ways, the engine was brought to new condition before being tested on a dynamometer engine tester. Meanwhile the 4-speed manual transmission was sent out to a specialty shop to be refurbished.

Seven full cowhides of English origin were purchased with contrasting Wilton carpeting and Stayfast canvas top material fitted to a padded top over the restored original top irons and frames.

As previously described, this car is constructed with steel rather than aluminum as was often used in coachbuilder cars of the period. Surprisingly, there was very little wood framing used to construct this body, a prevailing construction method of the era.

In short, everything was removed, inspected, fixed as necessary, or replaced as needed to maintain the excellent structural strength built into the body by craftsmen of Mulliners of Birmingham. The car was not only restored, but preserved in the process.

B342NZ's Chassis

CHAPTER 2

Sir John Black's One-off 1952 Bentley

"A thing of beauty is a joy forever, its loveliness increases." -- Keats

This most luxe and sporting car is the magnum opus of a lifelong restorer of 100-point Pierce-Arrows, Rolls-Royces, Mercedes, itself subject to an unstinting, every nut-and-bolt, four-and-a-half year, expensive restoration. Among a long line of previous success were a 1930 Phantom II All-Weather Tourer (convertible sedan) that won the Rolls-Royce Owners' Club Hooper Award, and a Pierce Arrow dual-cowl phaeton garnering Most Elegant Open Car Award at 1988's Pebble Beach. In its first outings, this handcrafted '52 Bentley beat a field of 460 cars to take home both Best in Class and Most Elegant Open Car at the 2014 Ironstone Concours d'Elegance, and the next month 260 cars at the Niello's Concours at Serrano, receiving both Best of Class and Best of Show. They are par, since three of Leon Garoyan's earlier cars took similar awards. Perhaps the touch of royalty miss out with the other of Garoyan's grand cars.

Once in a blue moon a single automobile comes along that embodies often disparate attributes: continental flair, the finest English coachwork, reliability, smoothness, and élan. Everything came together in this one-off, Mulliners-cloaked 1952 Bentley Mark VI drophead. The instant transformation from sophisticated luxury to debonair cache comes by lowering the disappearing top, a personality reinforced by the rakish split windshield that would do a classic Hacker or Chris Craft justice.

Better still, as a late Mark VI, this understated barouche is powered by the huskier "Big Bore," 4.6-liter (278-ci), dual-exhaust version of the tried and true Rolls-Royce seven-main-bearing B-60 F-head inline six, working through a smooth four-speed manual transmission, rather than the lurching HydraMatic with which most Bentleys bound for the US were saddled.

The Mark VI's top speed was an honest 106 mph, only 10 mph under the later, and less tractable, R-Type Continentals, unavailable as open cars.
Brakes were good for the day and still effective, being Rolls-Royce's power-boosted front hydraulic, rear mechanical drums.

We often hear such and such a car *"drives as well as it looks."* This one does.

The knowing gentleman commissioning this car was Sir John Paul Black, managing director of Britain's largest automotive manufacturing concern, Standard Motor

Company, supplying engines and transmissions to much of the Sceptered Isle's auto industry, Jaguar and Morgan among them. Black, overshadowed by American motoring moguls, was a business kingpin, lifting Standard from 1929's insolvency and 34 camshafts a week to 1951's 135,000 cars and Ferguson tractors, for sales of 47 million pounds ($122 million, or $1.1 billion in today's currency), helping take the postwar British auto economy to international levels.

Black so enthusiastically supported the British government's plan to adapt more efficient auto production methods to boost aircraft output as War II loomed, that he became Chairman of the Aero Engine Committee, for which he was knighted by King George V1.

 We've oft read that Detroit and the rest of our nation became "the arsenal of democracy," which was certainly true, but forget that England herself valiantly forged ahead against all odds, even as much of Standard's and Jaguar's Coventry was decimated by German bombs. Packard may've produced 55,523 Rolls-Royce Merlin supercharged V-12's propelling the fastest Allied pursuit planes, including the deHavilland Mosquito twin-engine fighter-bomber and four-engined Lancaster heavy bomber, but Rolls-Royce themselves delivered twice this amount during the war. John Black's Standard Motor Company built armadas of war material including 4,000 light armored cars, 750 Airspeed Oxford twin-engined trainers, 20,000 Bristol Mercury VIII engines, 3,000 Bristol Beaufighter fuselages, and 1,066 deHavilland Mosquitos.

Ian Fleming apparently took note of Sir John Black's one-off Bentley, since he put James Bond in one like this in his third novel, *Moonraker,* in 1955:

> *"The 1953 Mark VI had an open touring body. It was battleship grey like the old 4½ litre that had gone to its grave in a Maidstone garage, and the dark blue leather upholstery gave a luxurious hiss as he climbed awkwardly in beside the test driver."*

 In the early novels, Bond's one true love was his 1930 Bentley 4½ liter. After this was destroyed, he used his gambling winnings to buy a 1953 Bentley Mark VI with a coach built, two-door, open touring body, with the 4.6-liter engine.

Aside from availing himself of the best the English auto industry offered, John Black may have considered this unique Bentley a suggestion for a smaller sports car to compete in the booming export market already dominated by MG, Austin-Healey, Jaguar, and since his Standard organization introduced its successful, tractor-engined Triumph TR-2 in 1953. Observers noted the jaunty Triumph was nothing so much as a scaled down version of Black's personal one-off Bentley.

 Standard-Triumph merged with Mulliners of Birmingham, established 1897, one of England's last remaining coachbuilders, in 1958, after years of increasing control. The car's sole designer was Stuart Peck, who was brought to Mulliners through the aegis of the bespoke houses of James Young and Gurney Nutting.

Mulliners, Peck recounted, *"was renowned for producing well-built bodies in regular production batches at the right price but always to a high standard"* for many automakers, while the products of the separate H.J. Mulliner of Chiswick were subject on balance to more gentle treatment on usually professionally driven Rolls-Royce chassis. In the early '30s, Mulliners had simultaneously produced fabric over wood coachwork akin to Weymann bodies, a craft requiring enormous skill, all the more as such light bodies survived grueling venues like the 24 Heures du Mans.

What's novel in Sir John Black's '52 Bentley is the French connection. Peck was influenced by French carrossiers Henry Chapron and Giuseppe (Joseph) Figone, the latter employing dramatic two- and three-tone paint schemes. This smart, Gallic-themed Bentley's three shades of gray are true to its designer's vision. The soft symphony in gray is graciously complemented within by a lavish cockpit of burgundy, vat-dyed British leather, the dash and interior wood trim an entrancing "crotch burl with fiddleback" pattern by Madera Concepts of Goleta, CA, the official Bentley Motor Cars factory wood center in the US.

The convertible top is three-ply, square-weave Haartz Stayfast ensuring limousine silence at speed.

The authorized crest of Sir John Black on both doors is a small, genteel Knight's armor and shield; a car steering wheel designates Sir John's manufacturing status, a black raven signifies his family name. This bit of artwork is done in white gold. The minimal claret pinstriping is of unimaginable dexterity. There is not a glaring nor false note on this wheeled trifecta of earned nobility, inspired design and execution gliding on the most robust, refined chassis.

Underscoring the no-expense-spared nature of Sir John Black's open Bentley is that its unique, handmade body is crafted not of more easily handled aluminum, but steel, giving the strength and solidity of the best production closed cars. Advisors included his son Nick Black, Norman Geeson, technical consultant to the RROC, Tony Jenkins, registrar of the Mk VI & Silver Wraith Registry, Gerard Leclerc, Geneva, friend and founding president of the Rolls-Royce Enthusiasts' Club Suisse Romande (Swiss-French) chapter.

Locally, Roy Dryer, nationally renowned artist of classic cars and wood-classic speed boats advised with body colors. Tom Boutos, without question one of America's best body craftsmen studied the physics of the original body fabrication and re-bodied those panels needing such excellence exactly as done in 1952 in Britain.

A roll call of other veteran body men, painters, restorers, glaziers, platers, machinists, mechanics, spring re-archers, detail men and other specialists contributing to this rarity's rebirth would trivialize each. The plurals are intended, for when a pair of artists work in tandem, perfection becomes not a goal but realized. The sole veer from strict authenticity is the original radio's conversion to AM/FM while maintaining the face of its original controls.

More about Sir John and his Bentley

This is about a 1952 Bentley Mark V1 convertible coupe, B342NZ. Not just any Mark V1, but about a one-off design and creation, involving a British industrialist who was honored for services to his country by King George VI, and a design by what may have been an apprentice car designer, and its fabrication by a company that made bodies for cars purchased by the masses. A car that was in storage for over 38 years, completely lost from sight, and forgotten by professionals involved with keeping track of Bentley cars from the time they were each made. Seldom is there an opportunity to contribute to so many facets of history, long forgotten, that were at one time significant achievements. In some ways, it reminds us of the works of art by renowned artists whose works were "lost" during WW2 and were just being "discovered" in 2014.

Such is the fantastic epoch of the leadership of John Black as Managing Director of Standard Motor Company for the years between 1934 and 1954. During those years, and before, he served in the Royal Navy during WW1, afterwards the Royal Tank Regiment. During WW2 he provided industrial leadership and guidance to his country by marshalling the resources of the automobile industry, it's facilities, manpower, and skills to develop air superiority of the skies, long the domain of the Nazis. For that and other valued services, John Black was named a Knight by King George VI in 1943.

Following the Allied victory of the war, Sir John became concerned with developing a viable automobile economy, and concluded that efforts to design and produce sports cars for export may stimulate the post-war economy. Standard Motors were already supplying many smaller manufacturers with the drive trains for their cars, including Jaguar and Morgan, and about 10 or more others. His problem had three facets:

(1) Finding a suitable drive train.
(2) Designing a body that would compete with other sports car manufacturers on a global basis.
(3) Maintaining an aura of secrecy to not tip his hands to competitors, some of whom he had been supplying drive trains and other components for many years.

He purchased a Bentley chassis with 4.5 liter engine from Rolls-Bentley. This was a strong, well-engineered engine and chassis, widely acclaimed for its reliability.

Secretly, he considered Standard Motor's assortment of engines and drive trains that might serve as the engine for the sports car he intended to introduce. From several attempts, he found one he believed would provide the reliability and performance to compete with other sports cars. It is questionable that he ever considered the Bentley engine or drive train for his sports car, which was based on the TR2 models, abandoned shortly for the TR3 platform, with Girling front wheel disc brakes.

For his second problem he commissioned Mulliners of Birmingham to design and build an acceptable body for his proposed sports car entry. Records indicate Sir John actively participated in this endeavor.

Designing the body on the Mark V1 undoubtedly proved helpful for the final body on the TR2 chassis. In a sense, by building a body for the Bentley, the designers discovered what designs were possible to modify to the new Triumph. Some may consider the front wing design from the Bentley served as a proxy or proto-type for the TR2.

Thirteen months after the successful introduction of the TR2, his candidate for Standard's sports entry, Sir John sold the Bentley. It had apparently served its purposes. The Bentley had three owners in England, one of whom raced the car for 5 or 6 years. It remained in Great Britain for 10 years, before being exported to California in 1962. It's third owner in California decided to restore the car, but found his skills inadequate. He ultimately placed it in dry storage where it remained unattended for 38 years, until 2010 when it was purchased for restoration by its owner, Dr. Leon Garoyan.

To fully comprehend his purchase, the owner traced its history, much of it summarized above. He concluded:

• The history associated with the saga of Sir John, Mulliners of Birmingham as coach builder, and Stuart Peck as its main designer, and his one and only car ever, was worth preserving.

• Peck's designs embodying the work of the French school of car design warranted preservation of this car.

Moss Motoring article "Stuart Peck-Automobile Designer and Draftsman" relates:

"In 1951 Stuart Peck designed what turned out to be the last one-off body built by Mulliners other than prototypes for Standard-Triumph. It was built on a Bentley chassis which Rolls-Royce presented to Sir John Black of Standard Motors.

Recalls Stuart, "I was given a completely free hand and when I took the colored drawings over to Sir John Black he just said, "Yes, that looks great", so I took the full size drawings and supervised the building of the car which we delivered in Spring, 1952."

However soon after that Sir John was dismissed by his own directors and Alick Dick took over Standard Triumph. Just prior to this Sir John had indicated a desire to produce a competitor for the Jaguar XK 120 and that led to work started on the TR2 in 1952.

 As Stuart recalls: "Colonel White, who later became managing director of Mulliners, came into my drawing office one day and said: "Look Peck, I want you to go over to Coventry and talk to Walter Belgrove and Leslie Ireland because they are planning a 100mph sports car." It all sounded very exciting and when I went over, they already had the drawings of what became the TR2 and I brought those back to Mulliners to build the prototype. We weren't very keen on the bob-tailed rear, but after the Earl's Court show debut, Sir John rang Mulliners and asked us to design a new rear end. We took it on from there and did all the engineering for the TR range and I was put in charge of the TR Sports car section of the drawing office, becoming Chief Draftsman in 1956."

2014, showing the Bentley for its first hour at Pebble Beach Concourse d' Elegance.

Similarities can be seen here between the front fender design of the Mark VI Bentley and the TR3, both built by Mulliner. Walter Belgrove, designer of the original TR Prototype, would have known Stuart Peck who then joined him on the design team as Mulliner's Draftsman.

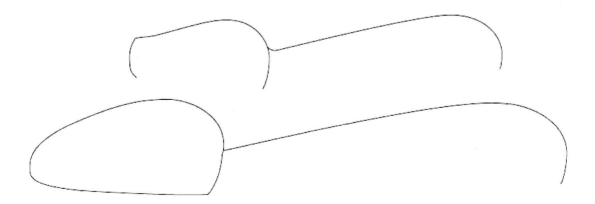

CHAPTER 3

The Concept of Natural and Self Endowed Management

From the beginning of my purchase of the 1952 Bentley Mark VI, I became an admirer of John Black because I saw the remarkable achievements with which he was credited.

Consider the industrial structure of the British car industry. Among those were two or three dominant manufacturers, that included Ford and Standard Motors each with about 7 reliable brands, plus several premium cars as the Rolls-Royce, Bentley, and a few others. There were a number of other competitors dominating the industry. Drop one bright industrialist with a sound education of finance, law and a large family with 6 males and two females whose father placed any two brothers into a "boxing ring" until they settled a dispute, and watch for the successful "way to solve disputes". Consider that as a tough solution for problem solving. That's a problem solving management system for success, and for a bright individual with a key mind, a good pattern for business management. John Black was a shoe-in winner. Toss in two appointments with the British Navy and Army and imagine the business advantages along with his human skills that provides a remarkable training ground.

I've had great respect for John Black as I heard about the family's problem solving procedure. Having a "boxing ring" method of problem solving probably led to effective decisions.

The period between 1929 and 1954 were exciting years of achievement for John Black and his associates. In 1934 he served as managing director when he brought the company into profitable operations. There were undoubted personal achievements in his life outside the operation of the company. His hiring of competent officials for Standard Motors enabled him to broaden other activities within the traditional scope of company activities: he made substantial expansion into selling automotive running gear to smaller competitors and observed their operations that gave him refinements of its own interests. His plans included concerns of how to expand Standard Motors into personal and sport cars, to help to maintain employment for the skilled personnel who had helped Great Britain and her Allies to defeat their enemies. The fantastic era of the John Black epic had been successful with great results.

While expanding the scope of manufacturing for Standard Motors, other smaller competitors were supplied with running gear which gave more car manufacturers the growth opportunities, ensuring the nation's auto industry the opportunity to change to advanced operating procedures that literally made them more successful.

He also made his own operations more successful, increased market expansion and became more involved in the fast changing market system that pleased car buyers.

Sir John's interests in fast sports cars was not a unique concept. The idea germinated in early 1930's as a response to such cars in virtually every nation. In the U.S. Ford developed the V8 Ford as an outgrowth of Ford, and virtually every production of Ford divisions promoted a "special" car.

This was the epoch training ground of Sir John's preparation for management:
- Tough personal decision makings.
- A quick response in assessing advantage or odds against him.
- Experience in negative advantages.

Repeat the above in terms of corporate decisions and you would be a believer of his successful management of public service, business acumen, and possession of success-based achievements.

John Black directed his family oriented cars into a reputable successful enterprise. His TR-3 became a car to improve quick starts and speeds, consistent with the wants of postwar car owners. He maintained a reputation of being able to meet the needs of sports-car type owners.

A substantial advantage was Standard's magnitude in size of production space, large numbers of skilled workers, access to capital over smaller fortunes, manufacturing and tooling equipment, skilled machinists, access to machines and government facilities and assistance. A clever executive with the above achievements and participation in public service had a positive advantage.

We have defined very significant personal characteristics, from family upbringing, public service, the nature of the public responses to national recognition of successful individuals, and other qualities common to Sir John Black as his personal strength and caliber. Combined with a close alliance with body maker Mulliners of Birmingham, together with the skills of Stuart Peck, strong economic and organizational ties were forged.

<u>Underscoring the Philosophy of Restorations</u>

Underscoring the no-expense-spared nature of Sir John Black's convertible Bentley is that its unique, hand-made body is crafted not of more easily handled aluminum, but steel, giving the strength and solidity of the production closed cars. Advisors included Sir John Black's son Nick; Norman Gleeson, technical consultant to both the RROC and the RREC; and Tony Jenkins, registrar of the Mark VI and Silver Wraith Registry of RREC.

Locally, Roy Dryer, nationally renowned artist of classic cars and wood-classic speedboats advised with body and interior colors. Tom Boutos, recently deceased, without question was one of America's best metal craftsmen, studied the physics of original fabrication and re-bodied those panels needing such excellence exactly as done in 1952 in Britain.

For a fortunate soul wanting a historic, vetted automobile of sterling provenance, crown jewel of British motors, cloaked in continental finesse; for someone who knows what it takes to produce the nonpareil, a timeless and lasting example of industrial art, this car must be seen.   The best talents were marshaled in its design and creation, as they were in its rejuvenation. To paraphrase Wordsworth, *"High is our calling, friend! Creative Art demands the service of a mind and heart, though sensitive, yet even in their simplest part, heroically fashioned."*

 The custom-bodied Bentley serial B342NZ is the pinnacle of a gentleman whose lifelong passion is the restoration of the world's finest vintage automobiles. This car has the added history of a renowned car industrialist, Sir John Black.
(Personal conversation between Mike Scott, Philosopher, Automobile Journalist, of San Francisco, California and Dr. Leon Garoyan, Classic Car Restorer and Collector.)

Body Restoration on B342NZ

CHAPTER 4

The History of the Bentley Mark VI and Early Owners

Sandwiched between the start of WW2 and England's successful victory with its needs to begin new efforts towards a peaceful economy, Rolls-Royce/Bentley came out with a new concept for cars to meet consumer interests.

The Bentley Mark VI was the lineal successor of the Derby Bentley of the 1930's and a traditional carry-forth of concepts to the Rolls-Royce Silver Wraith.

The Bentley Mark VI represented the first post-war generation of a luxury car designed for owner-drivers. Immediate steps toward economic development included plans for a new car to meet export markets to create jobs. It enabled them to view the future differently from their past.

Building bodies in their own factories created employment, made owner-driver cars easier to take care of because of standardization of body parts, increased the markets for their cars, and gave the factory more command of the marketing of its cars.

Prior to the war, the factory relied on independent coachbuilders to design bodies to place on their chassis. The Mark VI was a turning point from this practice, with the factory now building the chassis and bodies for their cars.

Of 5208 cars made between 1946-1952 only 20 percent were coach built, and Park Ward built most. This led to the factory eventually acquiring Park Ward.

Meanwhile the popularity of the Mark VI continued to grow and the waiting lines grew longer despite production efficiencies put into effect by the factory.

Significant Features of Sir John's B342NZ

There are three distinctions about this 1952 Bentley Mark VI four-passenger convertible coupe, each comprised by several features that make the car interesting for the public and for classic car collectors.
- Sir John Black, the industrialist who commissioned its construction.
- Mysteries surrounding the purposes for and uses of the car.
- Complexities of the car's restoration over a four-year period.

<u>Sir John Black</u>

Historically, the lineage of a car reflects its pedigree and gathers interests among viewers and collectors of classic and special interest models. Cars associated with entertainers, such as Elton John collect more aura than would the same model car originally purchased by an unknown. Likewise, the Pierce-Arrow owned by President Woodrow Wilson is displayed in a Museum that would likely not find an interest in the same model car owned by someone else.

John Black, the Public Servant

Sir John Black might have had a status of willing volunteer in the English economy. It is reasonable to consider as such, the magnitude of his roles of the major economies included were rampart - from automotive and vehicular, military including aircraft and armaments, recreational, undoubtedly for his personal enjoyment as a tension reliever.

During WW2 his workshops rose to the level of producing aircraft comprised largely of balsa, a type of lightweight wood with such strength that yielded bombers and fighter planes, effectively driving German aircraft from the skies. The Mosquito, also known as the "Wooden Wonder" could fly faster and further than any plane at the time while the enemy felt the impact in its rural regions engaged in military armaments. But with this unique warplane production, the enemy might have felt a moment of anxiety on how its rival, like a youngster, used balsa wood to fly toy airplanes! The British in charge of this operation were government and other officials who undercut their enemies fighting spirit. Sir John, as Chairman of the Joint Aero Engine Committee was in such government service. Also, the program was a credit at the time to the long-term reputation of British management skills.

Sir John Black was a Servant of the Nation, making substantial contributions during World Wars 1 and 2. He received Royal recognition for these periods of service, from the military and for his industrial support during critical years that faced England. Then too, he was a giant of an industrialist who led one of the largest English companies that built cars for the masses. Standard Motor Company, of which he served as Managing Director from 1934 to 1954, supplied smaller companies with engines, transmissions, and other components that served as an incubator for entrepreneurs who developed during the financially tough period of the 1930's. The companies that survived include Jaguar Motors and Morgan Cars.

His military tenure began as a seaman within the Royal Navy Department in August 1914; he rose in rank to the Machine Gun Corps and subsequent Tank Regiment, fought in major war zones overseas, and was wounded several times. Having been commissioned in 1917 he became one of the youngest Captains in the British army at his retirement.

In the intervening years between the wars, John Black held management responsibilities with a number of car manufacturing companies, beginning with Hillman Cars as the husband of Margaret Verena Hillman, daughter of William Hillman. Intertwined are years of employment with other prominent car manufacturers. In 1929 he joined Standard Motors, being selected as Managing Director in 1934, a post he held until 1954.

As threats of war enveloped Great Britain in the late 1930's, he served on various industrial commissions at the request of the Government. He provided industrial leadership and guidance to his country by marshaling the resources of the automobile industry, its facilities, manpower, and skills, to develop air superiority of the skies, for many years the painful domain of the Nazis. Such was the fantastic epoch of John Black as Managing Director of Standard Motors, worthy of screen action on its own. Playing a key role in the "Shadow Factory Scheme", he was one person in a whole team who directed the production of aircraft. Standard were also only one Company of many who were involved in the mass production of parts and components for aircraft. We know Sir John was knighted for his role, while the whole operation was run by the Government under the auspices of the Ministry of Supply with personnel like Ernie Bevin as Minister of Labour overseeing things.

Some refer to the Mosquito project as limited, in comparison to the Spitfire or Hurricane used in the Battle of Britain. But it served its purpose in a great variety of ways as fighter-bomber, night fighter, maritime strike aircraft and photo- reconnaissance aircraft, while dramatically boosting the morale of the British population. It was also evidently a joy to fly!

Sir John, the Industrialist

Sir John Black was the inspiration and drive of the Standard Motor Company as its deputy Chairman and Managing Director over a quarter century. After a few years with Humber and Hillman Motors, he continuously served Standard Motors from 1929 through1954, with amazing financial results. "From insolvency and thirty four cars made a week in 1929, he brought it to 47 Million Pounds Sterling sales from an output of over 135,000 cars and Ferguson tractors in 1951, three years before he retired.

"If history could be re-written in terms of achievement and industry rather than in terms of war and succession, it would be a work of the highest national importance. The times were ripe for it.

"It would teach the school children of today – the managers of tomorrow- that industry's battles are not less urgent because unsung, nor its defeats less calamitous in terms of national prestige and economy, nor its victories less inspiring because the territory fought over is measured in square feet instead of continents. It would teach the daily bloodless battles fought for empires far exceeding national limits, embracing the markets of the world. . …. by facts and figures and ruthless logic, the chaos and failure of bad or stubborn management, and of defeats turned to victory by guts and decision."

From *Sir John Black, Olive Moore,, Published by Creative Journals Ltd, 9 Grosvenor St. London and printed by Clement, Newling & Co. Ltd., Priory Works, Alperton, Wembley, Middx, U K.* 1951.

"Re-written on these terms, the Standard Motor Company, of Coventry, might well find itself rated as a public holiday, for in the industrial field its victories are resounding. Indeed, they are so numerous as to be confusing. *In each advance, success has been due to the general-ship of the man at the head who took over in 1929 when the Company was not only defeated, but in rout."* IBID. Emphasis added.

The Bentley MARK VI-Bentley's first post-war luxury car

Though considered a post-war concept, the Bentley Mark VI likely had its origins from the pre-war Derby models that had been successful cars of their time.

However, numerous changes in mechanical, suspension, chassis design, and exterior design were clearly related to the "new" Rolls-Royce Silver Wraith.

The Bentley Mark VI represented the first post WW-2 development of a luxury car designed for owner-drivers. Immediate steps toward economic development for Rolls-Royce/Bentley management included major changes by the factories, of which they:
- specified the owner-driver as the next stage in automobile ownership and use.
- shifted from major coach builder companies to factory constructed steel bodies.

The results were a major reemphasis in Company directions. Changing over to factory built standardized bodies extended access with owners, directly between the factory and the public. Overcoming the intermediary layer gave the factory a clarified relationship with the buying public and better control of the terms of selling their cars. It helped to stabilize the construction of bodies so that economies could be achieved within the factory. With standardized parts and panels, costs of repairs became less both in terms of labor and part costs. The concept of economies to scale developed in car ownership, so that the number of cars made and sold benefited the Company as well as the owners.

Technical Features of the Mark VI Models

Engine: Cars made from 1946 into 1951 were equipped with a 4 ¼ liter straight 6 engine (4,259 cc). In 1951 the engine was increased to a 4.6 L (4,566 cc/278 cu. In.) version that became known as the "big bore" engine. [B342NZ was made with the big bore engine.] The compression ratio was 6.4 : 1. Mark VI cars were rated as a 100 mph vehicle by The Motor magazine in 1951, and elsewhere as a 106 mph top speed.

Chassis and Running Gear: Rear leaf springs and independent coil springs at the front provide strong control, with a lever operated adjustment for changing the hardness of the ride hydraulically. A pedal operated Bijur lubrication system allows oil to be applied to moving chassis and steering parts. A 4-speed synchromesh manual transmission with the lever mounted on the floor is to the right of the driver.

Brakes: Drum-type brakes are fitted to all four wheels, with the front brakes being hydraulically operated and the rears are mechanical. The brake pedal operates the rear brakes directly, while the front brakes have a servo assist.

Wheelbase: In the beginning the cars had a 127 inch wheelbase, but from mid-1951 the wheelbase was increased to 133 inches along with an engine of 4,566 cc.

Tires: B342NZ is fitted to Coker Classic (radial) tires, 6.50 R 16 with Coker radial tubes.

Sir John's Industrial Achievements that Relate to B342NZ

Attributes of B342NZ are many and seldom found in an individual car:
- The story of the leadership contributions of John Black to the efforts of Great Britain during World Wars 1 and 2.
- His being honored by being made a Knight by King George V1.
- His contributions to the automotive industry as Managing Director of numerous marques and in supplying drive trains to other manufacturers.
- His help in the transition of the post-war British car economy to an international economy.
- The result of designing and developing a one-off Bentley convertible that is believed to have served as the proxy for the introduction of the later Triumph TR 3 which became a successful introduction and collector's item.
- The multiple of one-off status characteristics that add uniqueness to the car.
- The only post -war Bentley/Rolls made by Mulliners of Birmingham.
- The only car designed completely by Stuart Peck.
- The only post-war Bentley commissioned by Sir John.

Features of Sir John's One-Off Bentley

We believe Sir John did not commission the design of a new Bentley convertible to benefit Bentley/Rolls-Royce, yet we are unsure exactly why B342NZ was designed and built. The most likely reason is that, with the cessation of WW-2 evident, his concerns were on how to direct the resources and skills of Standard Motors to compete in the national and international pent-up demand expected to develop sportier cars than had prevailed before the war. He had made overtures to acquire several sports car manufacturers, Jaguar and Morgan, as examples, only to be rebuffed despite having supplied such car assemblers with drive trains for years before the War.

Before the War, Standard, and Mulliners of Birmingham, (the coachbuilder) had collaborated on designing and building a razor edge SS 100 Jaguar. Having acquired the Triumph Company after the War, it was natural to consider expansion of the Triumph resources as manufacturers of sports cars. In 1955, a year after Black's retirement, and with several years' attempts to test the market acceptance for Triumph sports cars at the Earls' Court Motor Show in London, the TR-3 was introduced, which received favorable market responses both within England and internationally. That model remains a collector's car to this day.

Chronological List of B342NZ Owners

One would think the matter of tracing the recorded ownership of a vehicle would be a straight forward process. After all, each change in ownership is always recorded with a government agency. In addition, there is a list of Bentley and Rolls-Royce car transfers maintained (sometimes provided on a voluntary basis by owners) by the Rolls-Royce and Bentley Enthusiasts Club in England, and its counterpart in the U S. the Rolls-Royce Owners Club (which includes Bentley car owners). In many ownerships, some of the transactions between owners may be found in files in museums, such as Warwick in England.

Graham Robinson to the Rescue

I was fortunate in receiving a response from Graham Robinson to my inquiry for ownership history made in *The Bulletin*, the publication of the RREC. Graham was a former 40-year resident of Bournemouth, who was now living in Bahia state, Brazil.

For months on end, Graham provided unbelievable factual information on each of the owners, including comments and information on survivors of these owners. I know of no such investigative source for the totality of Graham's investigative abilities. I have submitted all of the correspondence between us, including some responses from Nick Black, surviving son of Sir John in a later section of this history.

The Chronological List of Owners of Chassis # B342NZ; Engine # B171N

July 10, 1952	Delivered to Sir John Black
August 27, 1953	E.C. Poynter, Surrey
September 12, 1953	Robert Mercado Ltd. Leeds
September 1953	Leslie Onslow, Bournemouth
June, 1959	Jack Compton, (a Dealer), West Norwood, London
August 10, 1962	C. J. Gelber, Encino, California
1966	Sheridan Atkinson, San Francisco

April 27, 1973   Dr. Kurt G. Hammerstrom, Cupertino
October 10, 2010 Leon Garoyan, Ph. D., Davis, California
(Information about owners is based on Graham Robinson's Extensive Research.)

No one has seriously explained the motivations for Sir John to commission the design and construction of B342NZ. It is strange that Standard Motors had been supplying Jaguar with running gear for their Jaguar cars, including its sports roadsters since the early 1930's and continuing into early post-war years. The literature reports that he tried to buy the Jaguar Company to gain a sports car that he was well acquainted with, but he was rebuffed. Similarly, he had business relations with the Morgan family, and again he was unable to acquire that company.

It is obvious that Sir John was intent to have a sports car in his post-war offerings, and he had correctly determined that England and the export markets were ready for this emphasis.

The next question is why did he rely on a Bentley chassis when he failed to buy a line of sports chassis or use one from within Standard Motor's selections? It appears that he never did consider the Bentley chassis as standard for a car he would introduce. It is likely the Bentley chassis was a strategy to develop his sports model in greater secrecy. Perhaps the Bentley chassis provided flexibility, but a logical explanation could be the Bentley served as a prototype for testing design and performance criteria for Standard's new introduction. The Bentley running gear provided the type of motoring performance he wanted for his car, which left body design as the territory of testing consumer response. Randall Rich, a Sacramento based graphic artist who is also a car enthusiast, first pointed out to me similarities of the front fender designs between the Bentley and the early production TR-3 cars introduced two years later. The rear fender and spats design of the Bentley have similarities with the pre-war French school of design.

Some have suggested if Sir John commissioned the Bentley for use at Coronation Ceremonies for Queen Elizabeth in June 1953. They point out that Sir John was favorably thought of by the King and Royal family, and had served his nation admirably during two world wars. Aside from a photograph of the car in front of two pillars of an entrance to Windsor Castle, there are no other indications for such contention. Evidently, when not invited to the occasion, it is possible the Bentley had outlived its purpose!

The suggestion that the car was commissioned as a strategy for the involvement of Standard Motors in a new post-war entry into the sports car sector, through the Triumph reputation, bears heavily on why Sir John took an active role in the development of the car during its early planning stages. Some historians give low credence to this suggestion, even though the car was kept for only about 13 months after its delivery to Sir John by Mulliners of Birmingham.

On August 27, 1953 the car was sold to E. C. Poynter, of Surrey. Graham suggests Sir John had known Mr. Poynter for a long period before selling the car (A month later the car was sold to Leslie Onslow, a chap who reportedly raced the Bentley as well as an Austin-Healey and Mercury). Graham later picked up a reference to the person with the same name who raced cars at Le Mans.

See further http://marqueart.com/maquert/backgroundlemanshealey owner.htm, and http://www.grandprixmodels.com/articles/history/history03.pdf (See towards bottom of first column).

Mr. Poynter is recorded as owner for about one month before the car passed ownership to Leslie Onslow. We wondered if he was a dealer, but correspondence with Lance P. Poynter, a grandson, provides better information. In direct email, Lance states *"The swift sale of the Bentley may have been nothing more than the fact that the house in Fetcham had a small (narrow) entrance to the garage and it was off a narrow lane, so it may have been difficult or impossible to garage the car".*

Unless more information comes to light, this may remain one of several mysteries about the ownership of B342NZ.

Yet another small mystery is who was Robert Mercado, the person who bought the Bentley from Eric Poynter? The records are not clear. Robert's father was Maurice Mercado, who was naturalized in England in 1928. Apparently Maurice was from Spain? There is also reference in that same source to the Ottoman Empire, which was Turkey. That solves the puzzle as to why Robert changed his name from Yechava Salvator Beor Behar. Or does it? That he was either Spanish or Turkish, and he lived in Leeds is the best we can say.

Leslie Onslow is the next owner of the Bentley, having bought the car from Robert Mercado. Onslow seems to be the most interesting owner as described by Tony (Buzz) Onslow-Bartlett, his youngest son) and others who knew him. Tony had recently spent an evening talking about his family with his mother just before responding to Graham Robinson.

I quote from Tony's letter to Graham. *"Leslie was married a total of five times and enjoyed life to the full with a varied life, owning various car garages throughout the South Coast in and around Bournemouth/Poole area.*

"His fourth wife (Georgina (my mother)) met Leslie during the war on an airfield somewhere in the Midlands. Leslie was a chief engineer in charge of repairing the various fighters and getting them air worthy for the next day's sorties.

"Leslie enjoyed building and competing in various cars ranging from an Allard, Mercury V-8, Mini-Cooper, a MG, and others, including the Bentley. During his racing days, he was better known as "Bonzo". During his colourful career he had tried sheep shearing, was an accomplished paint artist, and in his early years he was a professional ballroom dancer, being paid to chaperone wealthy ladies to the London and surrounding ballrooms."

Caroline Onslow-Bartlett describes her grandfather as a *"flamboyant character".*

Records indicate Jack Compton, a London dealer, acquired the Bentley from Onslow in June 1959.

Graham Robinson 's inquiry with the authorities in Guildford, Surrey revealed that the JPB registration numbers were issued beginning in June 1939 - "So Sir John could well have obtained all 6 numbers when they were first issued and at that time he would have been well placed to do so". During the period when B342NZ was owned by Sir John, he'd had its registration as JPB 2. With its sale, the new registration became ODU 400.

Stuart Peck, the designer of the body, wrote that he preferred a two- color scheme for the car, but he was overruled by Sir John's preference for a black finish. The change to a two color grey combination was determined by C. J. Gelber who purchased the car for delivery to California.

On to The New World

The life of B342NZ in Great Britain seems to have been *exciting*, so one wonders why she would leave that interesting life. Perhaps the mysteries we have described during her early years were *too* exciting. Why was she **really** commissioned by Sir John Black? Were rumors of celebrating with Royalty over the coronation of a Queen too promising that they did not materialize? Or the sneaky , undercover manufacture to surprise her competitors too intriguing? Or had she not pleased her various owners that she was sent away? It seems she was so attractive that she was sent away to a different continent, for she next left England to make her new home in America.

The car had been exposed to the elements during its early history in England, and been actively driven, including racing by Leslie Onslow. Eventually it was perhaps a tired car, because the next owner had extensive repairs made as a condition of his purchase.

C. J. Gelber , of Encino, in southern California, bought her from Jack Compton, a car dealer of good standing in West Norwood, London in August 1962. In the following sections, we include the terms of the purchase. Gelber arranged for the car to undergo substantial repairs, including an engine rebuild, some problems with oil leaks, and even a change in exterior color. Documents to these repairs also appear in sections that follow, including correspondence between Gelber and Dr. Kurt Hammerstrom, its third owner in California. In the four years of his possession, Mr. Gelber drove the car regularly, amassing about 100,000 miles on the car.

- In 1966, Sheridan Atkinson, a financial consultant by profession in San Francisco, became its second owner in California. According to available records, the car was in his possession until April 1973, for a period of seven years. We are uncertain of the conditions of its maintenance. But there are indications it may have been exposed to the salt air of the Bay areas, as we attempted to understand where the car may have been exposed to adverse conditions that could lead to the serious body deterioration we observed, during the period of four years of the restoration it has undergone, at my considerable expense.

During the year of his occupation repairing the car, Tom Boutos, a metal craftsman from Sacramento, California, who first worked on the car for me, observed two types of repairs on the panels of the car. Being an astute forensic examiner on automobile damage as an expert witness, he hypothesized two styles of original repairmen who had made the repairs he was observing.

- One was the use of brass brazing to weld new metal panels, seldom used on quality repairs because the welds may become brittle and crack. He had placed the time period of those repairs to the period when the car was being driven by Leslie "Bonzo" Onslow, the flamboyant owner who raced cars aggressively. Later we found "Bonzo" had operated several repair garages in which he maintained the car after each race.

- The second type of deterioration observed was rust in unlikely locations, to be associated with salting of roads that would leave damage showing on the carriage of the under frame. Instead, the severe rust appeared on the upper and subpanels, as though the car had been exposed to a very salty atmosphere, such as found in the San Francisco area. We believe the major cause for our having to replace rusted panels by cutting and re-welding replacement panels required for quality repairs, occurred while Sheridan Atkinson's owned the car.

We surmise that such damage was observed by Dr. Kurt Hammerstrom within the first year of his purchase from Atkinson in April 27, 1973. Likely it was this discovery that led to his intended restoration of the car. But his frustrations with the magnitude of the body repairs required, induced him to store the car for 38 years in dry storage.

B342NZ as Found

Six months after his death, his widow, Molly, let it be known that the car was up for purchase. On October 10, 2010, I made that purchase based on estimates needed to restore the car. When I learned of Sir John's history of national contributions to his Nation and his achievements as an automobile industrialist in England, I decided to preserve the car through restoration and preservation.

Significant facts about Sir John and his Bentley Mark VI

The preceding has provided a thumbnail description of Sir John's public contributions as an industrialist during a period of two world wars that engulfed England. Time, and the personal life of private individuals, in contrast to public officials, tends to fade the public's memories of major contributions by individuals made for public causes. We believe this to be the case of the public with Sir John, whose national exploits for his beloved country appear to have faded over time. At the time of his relatively early death, the nation's mentality was concentrated on how to restore an economy devastated from a decade of war-time activities. This, much less than honoring an individual for his service to country.

In a foreword to a very readable book by Nick Black, the youngest and remaining son of Sir John, titled **Triumph and Tragedy,** John Macartney, whose father Charles was an employee and colleague of Sir John, refers to the problems of faded reputations thusly about him:

"But he was never forgotten by the many men and women whose careers he had helped to shape –in good times and in bad. To many of them, he was the icon of dependability . . ."

Sir John's life was not only interesting, but intriguing as well. From his "fairly humble background" his first marriage was to Daisy Hillman, one of six daughters of William Hillman, the motor magnate. After a tumultuous marriage he later married Joan, with whom he had three sons, before separating. Suffice it to say, his personal life was as interesting, but his marriages less permanent than his industrial life. The story of his life could be the makings of a soap opera or movie, while his service to country and as an industrialist could likely be more interesting for his contributions to "God and Country."

If the English public needs an individual to honor for his contributions to the war effort and the recovery period, the legend of Sir John could easily fill that bill.

Chassis Card Details

Rolls-Royce and Bentley clients may require specific details for the chassis they order from the factory. These requirements may be extremely specific, or generally similar, depending on the special desires of purchasers.

Presently many of the Build Cards are retained in the comprehensive files of the Rolls Royce (and Bentley) Enthusiasts Club and the information can be purchased from its headquarters at Hunt House in England. (Some of the build sheets in England have been copied and may be available from the RROC at its headquarters in the United States. They are included in this history of the car.)

The amount of information available varies; for some cars the information is extensive, and for others, it may be sparse. For B342NZ, the detailed information available from RREC is less than usual. We attribute that to the fact the car was built by Mulliners of Birmingham under quite restrictive arrangements with Standard Motors, located just outside Coventry. Sir John is believed to have imposed limited exposure to the design and construction of the body of B342NZ, for strategically competitive reasons. We are told that some of the data on the design and construction of the body was retained by Mulliners of Birmingham, as is typical for most cars they build. The strategic value or element of confidentiality is seldom important to an individual buyer, and may have benefits to a coachbuilder to make known its design and construction capabilities. Where there are strategically competitive reasons to gain a time advantage over rivals, there is a higher need for silence. We believe this to be a consideration with this Bentley. Incidentally, Mulliners earlier built a car for Sir John in secrecy during the war. Private correspondence dated 1943/44 between Colonel White, who later became managing director of Mulliners, and Mr. Thompson, who worked on the project, survive in the "Papers of the Standard Motor Company" now held at the British Motor Museum Library in Gaydon near Warwick.

Interior of B342NZ when first viewed October 2010.

The Build Card information for B342NZ consists of only four sheets, with many of the spaces open and do not contain information. These four sheets and two other sheets of information follow.

B342NZ's Modern History-More than a Face Lift

At first sight, there was no question that the car required a complete restoration. Though the fenders were attached, and the body seemingly intact, and the engine in place on the chassis under the bonnet, there was something ominous about the boxes of parts scattered in the main garage attached to the lovely Hammerstrom house. A trip through the house to the attic and the basement showed evidence of other parts. This Bentley was somewhat balanced between a basket case, and a car that had parts pirated. Eventually we determined the resurrection of the car was possible and desirable. That proved to be an optimistic opinion.

Goading us in this decision were two saloon-bodied cars, parked along each side of the Hammerstrom driveway, that were included in the sale of the convertible. One was very rough, and we thought the other mostly good as a parts car.

It required three trips to haul this assembly to start the restoration process.
As the photos indicate, the undertaking appeared feasible, but substantial.
We sanded the red oxide cover that had faded during storage, but we soon realized more vigorous methods would need to penetrate the years of accumulated material to reach the metal. What became obvious was that the metal work required would only be evident by aggressive bead blasting, made necessary because inner panels were sometimes in worse condition than the exterior metal. This alerted us to the probability that we had uncovered several types of metal damage, some by apparent accidents that had been improperly repaired, while the hidden rust damage was more likely the cause of extensive years of exposure to salt air, common to climates near oceans. Finding the rusted areas required two bead-blasting treatments in the worst of the body regions where atmospheric salt air could penetrate even tightly concealed body areas.

There was no rust problem on the frame, indicating the steel frame had not been exposed to road salts.

The body was lifted from the chassis, to enable us to concentrate on cleaning and powder coating the chassis and all components attached to it. The engine, transmission, radiator, springs, and all steering system, front and rear suspension work were made to new standards, including even spring shackles, which were remanufactured to factory specifications provided by Norman Geeson, of England.

At this time, I had retained Tom Boutos, a nationally regarded metal repair authority to repair the body. Tom worked for 13 months in his private Sacramento shop to trace rusted steel panels, removing rust by cutting, re-forming new replacement steel, and re-welding the newly fabricated panels. The results were excellent.

The body next was taken to Lee's Vintage Car Shop (no relation to Lee Garoyan, the car's purchaser), to finalize the body alignment and to prepare the body for its primer coats, in preparation for final fitting of panels and colors. The time had come to return the car from Hayward to West Sacramento, when a tragic error occurred that allowed the car to partially break loose inside a trailer. At least 4 months of work had been destroyed in that accident, causing loss of time and money. Ultimately, that problem was repaired, and a very complicated paint pattern was begun. Lee's Car Shop had the car for 15 months for these activities.

The car was shuttled to and from Hayward several times and finally returned to West Sacramento for fitting of glass to windows, doors, and other items, including 3-D manufacturing of rubber window seals.

Meanwhile work had progressed on the final trimming of the interior of the car, such as cutting and fitting of new English leather to front and rear seats, and final selection of the top material to complement the complex paint scheme designed by Roy Dryer, an internationally known car and classic wood boat artist.

In all, over 12,000 man-hours were involved with the restoration of the car since I acquired it in October, 2010.

B342NZ in Tom Boutos' Workshop

CHAPTER 5

Mark VI Bentley Cars: A Model That Changed the Company

The Mark VI was introduced in 1946 with production ending in 1952 with more than 5,208 cars produced, mainly in Rolls-Royce factories. The decision to produce standardized bodies led to other major changes for the company:

- relying on Park Ward as a more important factor in design and production,
- more emphasis on owner-drivers as customers,
- standardized steel bodies, with fewer individual custom cars,
- broadening its market base.

Coach built cars were available too, but in much fewer numbers. While 520 factory steel bodied Bentleys were made, there were only 1018 coach built Mark VI produced. H. J. Mulliner produced 307 of them, followed by James Young, Park Ward, and Freestone and Webb. Of the total coach built cars, 806 were made by these four largest builders, accounting for 94 percent of total coach built cars. Of these, only 181 drop-head Mark VI coupes were made. Sir John's car is a rarity among rare cars.

Technical data are available elsewhere, that indicate that the early production of Mark VI was made with a 4.3 liter engine, and in 1951 after chassis B2MD, a big bore engine was used, with 4.6 liter. This resulted in improvements of speed and performance. (B342NZ is one in which a big bore engine was a factory item). The resulting cars fitted with larger bored engines were powerful, faster, and able to more than hold their own on the improved motorways. They were rated at top speeds of 106 mph.

The story gets interesting

It has been noted that the Bentley Mark VI represented the first post WW2 development of a luxury car after many years of war. Immediate steps toward economic normalcy for the U. K. included development of an export market to earn capital. The automobile industry became a major priority for both the British nation as well as for reverting car manufacturing facilities from wartime production to a peacetime economy.

That strategy was successful and the car manufacturing industry began to move from making staid family cars to more sports and personal cars; many of these cars were successful and remain as collector cars to this day.

It is from this background that B342NZ history began. The car remained with Sir John only briefly, about 13 months when it was sold to its next owner in the U. K.

This lends credence to those who believe B342NZ served as a prototype for development of a sport car to be made by Standard Motors, and that sport car became eventually the TR-3. Obviously Standard Motors would not be able to make bodies using Bentley running gear; however, Sir John had experienced internal hesitance from some Standard Motors board members, which likely resulted in the one-off production of B342NZ as a prototype.

There were two more owners in the U. K. before C. J. Gelber of Los Angeles purchased from Jack Compton Ltd in 1962. Four years later Sheratin Atkinson of San Francisco purchased the car, and in 1973 Dr. Kurt Hammerstrom of Los Altos became the third U. S. owner.

News of a "barn find" spreads

A "barn find" remains a hope of many collectors. This car's "find" was slightly different. After the death of Dr. Kurt Hammerstrom, his widow contacted a prominent RROC-Nor Cal region member with news that her deceased husband's car would be for sale. Being located in the Bay Area Region of San Francisco, in Los Altos, a city about mid-way between San Francisco and San Jose, the RROC member contacted upwards of 30 members, many of which showed interest in the car. Few members knew of the car's existence in their vicinity. The car's owner had placed it in dry storage after his attempt of restoration had begun, and ended, with the car partially dismantled. Since the car remained in this condition for 38 years, its re-emergence in 2010 was major news within Bentley circles. No one recalled its existence in California; in the U. K. it was also a forgotten reality, since it had only been registered there for 10 years.

The news of its re-emergence spread slowly, first in the Nor Cal region of the RROC, and then on the national scene. Within six months, I reported its purchase to Nick Black, the son of the original owner in England, and word eventually spread as it has emerged, which indicates the significance of this car find and an important part of European post-war automotive history.

Factory Bentley Cars in Transition, Post WW2 to Present

It is difficult to compare car models over time regardless of criteria used. Recently I was compelled to do that for a one-off Bentley Mark VI convertible. This is the first luxury post-WW2 model F chassis and the only one with this type of body.

Mark V1 models had interesting characteristics in their manufacturing process. With previous models, coachwork was produced by a large number of specialized coach builders independent of the Bentley factory. But beginning with the Mark VI that function was internalized with good corporate results.

Alan Judd wrote an interesting article in the Spring 2016 issue of Bentley magazine titled *Transport Delights* that illustrates the difficulty of rating the innovations of driving the modern Mulsanne Bentley model "with its beguiling power and comfort" in comparison with its earlier year's productions. One would conclude the modern Mulsanne is so different from its earlier issues it cannot be meaningfully compared with each other. Yet that was the task I was required to do for the 1952 one-off Mark V1.

I am a car enthusiast who buys for a car's future value and my tendencies to own a car for its "at-time" appearance at the purchase time. In a sense I value a used collector car looking backward to its past models. Lets' take what factors come into my equation.

I own a 1952 Bentley Mark V1 convertible whose value is likely based in part on significant differences if it is compared with like-cars of this model. Since there is no other car like this, and there never will be; the problem is difficult and mute.

The car was commissioned by Sir John Black, the Managing Director of Standard Motor Cars, as a prototype for a new sports car to be built. Some wonder if it was built to serve as a new car for Sir John to participate in social activities concerning events at the coronation of Queen Elizabeth. Sir John had been honored by King George V1 for his role as war-time chairman of the Nation's aero engine committee that converted automobile resources to construction of aircraft. Some of Standard Motor's facilities were converted to this purpose, and produced 1,066 Mosquito bombers to destroy the enemy war factories.

Adding to its value are the car's design characteristics- a rare application by designer Stuart Peck of French influence of Henri Chapon, and Joseph Figone, well-known Continental car designers. The French influences are recognized as the flowing wings from the front; past the door configuration to an ending at the rear wheel housing at the rear wheels. Here the rear wings attached to the body and the boot panels are characteristic of French designers.

Stuart Peck next added other French touches, and value, such as the split windscreen glass, and the well into which the canvas top is placed below the rear deck when the car functions as a convertible. This well neatly serves as a safety item, since the top's resting on the rear deck would partially obstruct the view of traffic from the driver's seat.

The car's exterior colors are also a rarity made possible by the body's exterior lines. There are no exterior chrome strips often used by car designers to break up the side exterior panels. No other Bentley of this model has body lines as produced on B342NZ, but several builders adopted the car's features into their production of their R-type Bentleys that followed the completion of this car.

Finally, the internal space shows details that highlight the car's interior with the unusual exterior design. The use of natural and rare wood trim and the interior leather seats and color adorned leather seat piping coordinated with wool carpets assure the car will maintain its high values consistent with its one-off rarity.

Alan Judd describes similar features that make the Mulsanne Bentley a "Transport of Delight", a blend of engineered features that add to "the car's sheer maneuverability" and "road manners compel a style of driving that is considerate and decisive". Judd poetically suggests characteristics that have made the Bentley the "car of the period regardless of the period compared." I understand.

The door panels show a rare interior combination of several shades of red leather with contrasting trim. The same color combinations are featured on each side panels where a gray wool pleating provides a unique finish. The wood trim on the doors and dash is notable since it has a combination of two layers of different types of wood, one design is Crotch Burl with Fiddleback, a distinct pattern not often available, surrounding the natural wood. The door panels feature a Sunburst design that is unique to this car.

Apropos the 1952 Bentley Mark V1, one off convertible coupe with its 4.5 L. engine, completely preserved to honor Sir John Black, whose service to country and sports car enthusiasts remain to be in our memories.

From Restoration to Preservation, Completed in About Four Years

With slightly more than 38,000 miles showing on the odometer when I acquired the car in 2010, the thoughts of a fast restoration seemed reasonable. Since the car was partially dismantled, the first effort was to wash the years of accumulated dust, and to lay out the parts obtained in boxes to determine how complete the acquisition was. Remarkably, most parts were located, so our emphasis turned to determining the status of the body. After washing, we decided to remove the paint by chemical stripping by hand, and what appeared were sheet metal repairs that indicated a need for further assessment. Strangely, evidence of rust showed too, but in higher regions of the body instead of areas subject to road salts. This was perplexing, so we decided to have the body power-stripped inside and out. Having done that, we now realized these were rusted areas on the undersides of the steel panels, so we needed to remove the body from the chassis, and to start anew with this restoration.

At this point, we faced a major decision: we could trash the body, make a special body and change its original design. Had we made this choice, the car would no longer be Sir John's car. Alternatively, we could bite the bullet and preserve the car to its original stature. We opted for preservation, for reasons described in prior pages that indicated the unique characteristics of the car.

It took 50 weeks (of 50-hours each) of effort by Tom Boutos, a highly skilled and nationally recognized metal craftsman to cut, trim, fabricate, weld, and otherwise rebuild the body to its original dimensions. Photos in subsequent pages of this document indicate the thorough nature of this work.

With the body off, the frame went to a R-R factory trained mechanic and restorer to prepare the chassis and all mechanical components of the car. The frame was powder coated, the Bijur oiling system was made operational; the engine, transmission and all drive train components were rebuilt; carburetors were rebuilt, and virtually all of the work of the frame was made as new. All instruments were rebuilt; steering wheel refinished; new old stock body hardware obtained from the U.K.; new glass installed; and every moving component of the car repaired and refinished.

New suspension system components were acquired or rebuilt from factory machinist's specifications and drawings. The rear spring were rebuilt to original specifications.

There is very little wood framing on this car, but where damage existed, new old-growth kiln-dried ash was obtained for replacement.

After metal fabrication, the body was removed to Lee's Vintage Car Shop for metal surface preparation, priming to protect finished metal, and application of the final color coats of paint. This turned out to be a ten-month project.
All paint materials are in strict compliance with the most stringent California environmental laws, considered to be the toughest anywhere.

Highest quality leather for seats and door panels, canvas top material and wool carpeting originating from the U.K. were installed by Biner's Upholstery. Coker radial tires and tubes are mounted on the powder coated factory wheels.

The final paint color selection was made with the assistance of Roy Dryer, a consultant and professional artist who specialized with classic automobile and wooden boat subjects. The color scheme was selected to enhance the contours and raised metal highlights, to reveal natural divisions of the body originally designed by Stuart Peck with that in mind. Peck's recommendations for the original color scheme is largely followed by the three shades of gray recommended by Roy Dryer, as indicated in the artist's rendition.

Once acquired and then missing, B342NZ's emergence stimulated renewed interest. Like a rare work of art that received collector acclaim and then disappeared from sight and was never heard about since, the Bentley was a "new find" in the U.K. and among collectors in the United States. Gone from sight by being placed in storage for 38 years, memories of the car were mainly registered in Bernard L. King's book "Bentley Mk VI" with minor reference on page 272. Sir John's son, Nick Black's comments were that they thought the car had been destroyed.

Likewise, TR-3 clubs in Holland and England picked up on the prototype aspects of the front wing design similarities of the Bentley's wing design to the application on the TR-3 front wings.

The forgoing story features the history of a unique car. What is its future and whose names shall be entrusted to perpetuate its potential in ways that have not yet been exploited? In a sense, that is the ultimate decision to be made.

Mulliners Ltd.

Founded at Birmingham in 1887 by Henry Mulliner, who was related to both Arthur and H. J. Mulliner, the company ceased to operate in the early 1920's. During 1924 the name and goodwill were purchased by Louis Antweller. Under his leadership the business flourished, mainly building on the medium sized chassis for local car manufacturers. Standard and Lanchester. He also built eighteen Rolls-Royce 20HP; 24-25 HP; 4 each of the new Phanton II and Wraith.

The close working relation between Sir John and Mulliner is significant when Sir John turned to Mulliners to develop the Bentley Chassis B342NZ as his prototype for the TR-2 and then TR-3 as his successful sports cars.

Another coincidence was that Stuart Peck, who worked with Mulliners coach design was chosen as Sir John's main designer for his personal prototype. Stuart Peck, also draftsman for the TR range, did not move far but he did move considerable distance by bringing substantial body style changes to British car design.

CHAPTER 6

First Views of B342NZ, October 10, 2010

I was among the first members of the Rolls-Royce Owners Club of Northern California to view the 1952 Bentley; none of us had seen the car and we were unfamiliar with what to expect.

As we looked at the vehicle, the worst we could envision was it had been dismantled by someone else, and we didn't know how many items may be missing. As you see the photos that follow, try to overlook the accumulated dust of 38 years; the exterior panels appeared to be in good shape. The most distressing view was of the interior, but we would have to replace most of that segment anyway. Based on this inspection that took several hours, I became interested in purchasing the car and decided to do some quick budgeting. The budgets looked favorable, too.

It was after I had won the bidding to buy and got beyond the old primer coat that had been applied sometime longer than 38 years ago that we realized the magnitude of the work to be done to bring the car to quality standards that the car merited, and that met our prior experiences.

Our options were to:

- limit our restoration to the car mechanically, and to engage in a cosmetic exterior make-over. We have seen such restorations, but not done one ourselves.

- replace the body with a "Bentley Special" as we have observed at Club functions.

- part out the car by selling components.

- Proceed with further probes into the metal to determine the extent of body damage and remanufacturing the panels that required replacing.

We decided for the last option, which required hiring a metal craftsman to fabricate new body panels, a process we had not encountered in prior restorations. We learned that King George VI had honored John Black a Knighthood for significant public service, so that influenced our decision. The design of a one-off car with unusual and attractive contours further influenced us.

The fact that the design was the first and only car that Stuart Peck had ever designed to completion from stem to stern was challenging for its special body. Combining all of these circumstances led me to proceed, recognizing that Sir John's achievements for his country was a challenge worth making known and celebrating, 60 years later. Its provenance was appealing.

In the pages that follow, we provide the reader an in-depth understanding of the joys we shared, the concerns and discouragements we encountered, and the thrills we felt. When completed, we believed we would present a car as strongly built as originally by Mulliners of Birmingham. We stuck to authenticity, deviating only when improved technology or materials improved strength or safety. Even while work progressed we received comments from those who have watched the process of restoring and preserving a car deserving of the attention we believe was justified. We believe the memories of Sir John as a national hero would become rekindled for both the people for whom his services were provided, and for the post-war leadership he contributed to car enthusiasts who enjoy sportier cars.

B342NZ as first seen.

My first view of B342 NZ was in October in 2010. These first had to be rapid as time was limited and the temperature was freezing in San Francisco. Within a year of reaching out to new visitors sojourns new guest was winning commendations in many compliments or views.

Delicacy comes with age and relevancy. Seldom are joints considered things of beauty such as the angles and curves as shown in the fusion on this car. Imagine how such fusion forms joints, welds and added strengths combined with curves as only this Stuart Peck design exhibits. He was a generation ahead of current body design, conceiving of the mystical blend shown in B342NZ.

Lee and Nina Garoyan with B342NZ

CHAPTER 7

Skills of A Metal Craftsman

Aside from the frame and the supporting structure imposed on it, a car's strength derives from the wood and metal that embrace the physics of constructing a moveable object that is exposed to twisting and bending, with vertical and horizontal thrusts which influence the mass of steel and wood that comprise the body. Tom Boutos was the metal craftsman who made sure the car would withstand the hazards to which it is tested; he judged the original body designed by Stuart Peck and constructed by Mulliners of Birmingham as a "very strong design". I am not sure how long it took Tom to reach that conclusion, but he spent about 12 months fabricating the metal and wood of B342NZ.

When Tom got to the metal of this car, he found it was of steel construction except for the rear boot door, which was made of aluminum. As he progressed panel by panel from the exterior in to the sub-panels he was like an archaeologist/anthropologist able to describe damage whether from driving, rust from atmospheric characteristics of where the car had been situated as compared to road salts, and the experience and skills of those who worked at Mulliners and those who had made the repairs. Nearly daily he sent me photos of the panels he had worked on, what he had found, and what corrective repairs he had made of prior repairs. With information from Tom's observations and the descriptions of the car's owners and occupations, we tentatively identified that Leslie "Bonzo" Onslow was likely responsible for body damage as a result of his racing of the car, and its exposure to salty marine air on the south coast of England, which probably accounted for rust. The second exposure likely came from the ownership by Sheratin Atkinson, who lived in the coastal San Francisco Bay Area, a likely contributor of a salt air environment.

In the photos that follow, we show typical types of rust and bad repairs that had plagued the car, and the ways that were used to cut metal badly laced with rust. Likewise, moist conditions contributed to development of wood rot. Because photographs show typical types of rust and corrosion, we substitute several half-page views.

Two other pictures show that the lower parts of the door panels had rusted out and required replacement. Panels were cut, and replacement metal fitted and welded to fit the metal removed. Another photo shows the bottom portion of the door after it was repaired. In compatibility, two metals may be chemically unable to fasten or heal.

Wood and Rust renovation

No part of the car was free of rust, even panels on upper levels of the body, due largely to the high concentrations of atmospheric salts in the air. The third picture shows the right rear quarter panel, removed from the car to enable access to the required work. The dark areas of the quarter panels are metal that were cut and replaced.

There was only moderate use of wood in the car, and we replaced it only when necessary. We used kiln dried clear ash wood obtained locally from Sierra Nevada Mts. And milled to our needs by a Sacramento specialty supplier with a sawmill operation. Most of the damage to wood was due to moisture, mostly in regions where moisture accumulated and remained wet. The above pictures show the exposures of wood in the framework in conjunction with metal. It seems we may have added to the original strength when we replaced wood by use of steel wood screws plus improved glues now available.

The frame for the spare tire door was made new, later shaped and covered with new metal.

The wooden curves mirror the beauty of the rear fenders.

A mystery of strength is undeniably its quality of beauty, because from beauty comes purity that is seldom achieved nor asked, nor shared. Such strength shows in the pillars and the double beams in the photos above. The capability of the craftsman is exhibited by the combined effect of the contours double panels that Tom Boutros decided we needed for strength that used the interaction of steel and the virgin wood. This saga of design seldom appears from the combined work of a designer such as Stuart Peck, and Tom Boutros as a re-creator of Peck's design.

Personal Experience about Rebuilding the Bentley

The dismantled Bentley came into my life on October 10, 2010 in a message that left me excited. I had not heard of this car that had been in dry storage for 38 years, and as active as I had been in Rolls-Royce and Bentley, local, national and international club activities, I received the news of the car's availability with awe.

I went to the storage area the next day by arrangement, and visited the intriguing house address given to me.

It was a sad story for Molly, the widow at home, whose deceased husband had bought the car about 38-40 years earlier and after enjoying several years of touring with the car had decided to restore it. He started to dismantle it unaware of its technical complexity. Work became very complicated, so he took over the family car garage space, and eventually that space was fully occupied with a non-operating vehicle. Gradually that became the status of the vacant basement also. I stood sadly taking in the scene and thoughts. I wondered if all the parts were available and in what condition? And Molly was wondering if I could restore it or was I on a "curiosity" trip?

I was back the next day by agreement with Molly, with a friend who often did mechanical work on my Rolls-Royce and Bentley cars.

No one living in California while this Bentley was being offered knew who the car originally belonged to except, "He was a Titled Man". It would not have impressed any of us to know it was ordered by John Black, or that Stuart Peck had served as its sole designer. To us, it was a well-worn Bentley with interesting, well curving bodylines, but well used. "John Black? I do not know the man". Nor was the car dismantled in the garage visible from the street, so few had seen the car by peaking.

I bought the car that second day and it took two days to haul everything to a shop where we began to wash all its extensively covered soil and dirt.
We took our notepads and camera and started to estimate the car, components, status and evaluation in cartons, etc. Oh yes, and the replacement value (despite appearance we found

everything would be replaced if I restored the car). We didn't know if the price for a part was available, or if available at all to estimate repair costs. We also did not know if the car was a factory specimen costing thousands of dollars, or if the sheet metal was a private design, or if this body was an all steel body by Mulliners of Birmingham made only for this chassis. The local parts shops could not help us. The fact the chassis and running gear was Bentley was only partly helpful, and some components had special order parts.

Give us a sample you say? This Bentley has rear chassis-body leaf springs that were not available anywhere in the Bentley parts system, that are specially made and the Bentley-Rolls warehouses are empty, but the factory gave us the blueprints, and reported the specifications for the steel are from a small machine shop in India.
Richard Treacy of Australia came to our rescue with contracts and acquisitions, and located a machine shop in Australia to manufacture the pins and other components for me and they fit "as new".

In the washing experience, some indication of the car's condition emerged, so a removal of the old paint and body primer was undertaken down to the steel body. We expected to deal with rust, since a magnet would not always stick to the body, indicating layers of body filler. Many of these coach-built cars had aluminum bodies, but B342NZ was all steel except for the trunk lid, which was made of aluminum.
Hand stripping the old finishes was an important step to understand the history of the car. It revealed a complex set of problems including the location of prior damage, a useful indication of structural weaknesses requiring correction, if any. What we found in B342NZ were several collision damages, but none of which were structurally significant. Earlier, when we had taken the body off the chassis for cleaning, we noted no structural problems with the frame, and simple tests showed it to be straight. We found other conditions of improper repairs, with failures that were corrected with new repairs overlaying the earlier repairs. Also, there were repairs made with brass brazing that had broken. Hand stripping chemically of old finishes was considered necessary in many cases.

Hand stripping had weaknesses too. It is best for examining the exterior of the car body, but with many cars, there are secondary panels that are difficult to reach with hand stripping. Because of the problems with the integrity of earlier damage, we had the car completely blasted with plastic media, including both sides of the body, and interior parts that were not accessible previously. That revealed metal etched like filigree designs from continuous exposure to salts, in areas not associated with salt from roads. The stripper offered to spray a coating of zinc on both sides of the body that could be worked with files to fill all the body that was damaged by salt, and which would fill all of the filigree in the process. Unfortunately, that would not repair the rusted out metal that needed to be replaced to maintain structural strength. In addition, there was a considerable amount of wood framing on the body and doors, that would need to be replaced and refitted.

At this stage of our decision making, I relied on Tom Boutos, my metal craftsman, for guidance and that may have influenced the decision to proceed as we finally did. Tom is an artist with very narrow tolerance for opinions that challenge his experiences. He has broad experience in crash repairs including frame repairs, progressively to the construction of new bodies on rare (and expensive) cars, and preparing the body for final paints and applying the paints. There is not anything in reality, that he has not done with a car, and done successfully.

I relied on his opinions after discussing options with him. Perhaps some combination of total replacement and zinc coating would have worked, but that was not the option for most matters of importance.

A few times we had serious differences in opinion, and we talked them through to a mutually acceptable solution. Once he threatened to withdraw unless we did something his way, and I asked, "that if I listened to him, would he listen to me" which he did. We found we were explaining the same "result" in different professional language. On one occasion, near the conclusion of the metal work, Tom suggested I find someone else, I told him no divorces were allowed at this stage, we would have to work out our differences. We did.

Tom set the schedule for the work on this car, not necessarily the critical path, a term we both understand the meaning and implication of, but the time schedule. There were four other specialist seeking access to the car, but access was established by Tom's speed and sequence of accomplishing a task. He, at this schedule, had now held the car captive for nearly a year, and we both knew it was time to let it move on. I sensed a reluctance on his part, and I finally asked him to work out a strategy to work on the few bits of work remaining for him to complete, and to pass it on. After a year in possession, I sensed he had a possessive feeling for the car. He liked the challenge and admired the car's design.

Tom Boutos- Thinking about B342NZ

First Effort in Restoring the Body Was Wrong

Our first assessment of what it would take to restore the car was based on observations right after the hand stripping of the paint to expose bare metal. This first assessment was based on inadequate information and faulty conclusions. Because we underestimated the true condition of the metal, we made the wrong decision as to the skills needed. As a result, we lost a month's efforts in the project, and several thousands of dollars in money. That's when we realized the magnitude of underestimating the condition of the car we had decided to restore, which was to cost us dearly in time and money. Based on our earlier assessment, I had been invited to apply for the 2012 Pebble Beach Concourse scheduled in mid-August. By then, the car was with Tom waiting for completion of body restoration.

In all, the body was with Tom for 11 weeks in 2011, and 35 weeks till August 10, 2012. I expect we used two, and possibly three more weeks before Tom released the car for others to take over. He did remarkable work to preserve a body that was so far damaged by rust and bad repairs early in its life. The repairs and reconstruction of new panels far exceeded our estimates and prior experiences in restoring a car. By then, he was expected to have finished all reconstruction of metal repairs, which we found was an impossible date to meet.

This is a unique system for restoring a car; more common may be to have the work being done under one shop location, but ours involved several shops.

Certain few employees, until our team learned, adjusted to the routine and corrected for their early-on work issues. I met the problem early on of inadequate planning because of Tom's brilliance, education, and work capability. He was a take charge person by experience and had my admiration for quality work. The group got together in late July with good results.

Our team was highly impressed with the quality of work done by Mulliners of Birmingham, the car's builder, and Stuart Peck designer, as to their quality of work and materials used. We were amazed at the poor quality of maintenance and repairs by some of the intermediate owners who caused serious body damage while owned by them that later required corrective repairs by my team.

CHAPTER 8

The Colors of The Car

Stuart Peck recommended a paint pattern of black and grey but Sir John overruled him. The car was painted entirely black. That may have been a symbolic consideration for his surname, "Black".

There are only four original pictures of this car that we have been able to locate; the photos are as scarce as the car is rare. None of the pictures reproduce well, but they were all still black as order by John Black.

Few of the subsequent owners in England objected to a black Bentley convertible, unless it was sold to an American, whose one of several requirements was repainting the exterior of the car "grey", and with maroon leather upholstery. This was a requirement of C. J. Gelber, in 1962 when he purchased the Bentley from Jack Compton, Ltd.

Prior to my sale of this Bentley, we researched over long periods to determine the combinations of colors that showed the car best to achieve the most recognition. We wanted the best appearing length, an image of speed even while parked, harmony, and sleek to the ground. From this research we concluded these resulted with three shades of grey, and the color of a red Napa wine I had made several years earlier as body accent trim along the door margins, bonnet and wheel trim.

The appearance of length to the car, and less of a "bulky" effect is important. The change in paint scheme added to its sleek, sporty appearance, and is consistent with the concept Roy Dryer, the color designer for all of my quality classic cars, wished to project with this car.

> My objectives for paint colors:
> 1. achieve a lengthy appearance to the car,
> 2. a concept of speed, even when parked,
> 3. harmony in appearance of body,
> 4. low image to the road,
> 5. achieve a paint scheme that harmonizes the owners' feelings of wealth, prosperity and "classy".

We painted 120 paper images of the car with color combinations to best achieve the desired characteristics. We concluded a combination of dark grey on the wings, with a moderate grey over, and with a bluish grey on top gave us our desired results. A paint color to feature a Napa Cabernet from my productions served as a trim highlight, covered with a grey canvas top achieved the outer results.

Roy Dryer's display of different color combinations.

Consider These the Fine Points of Beautifying A Car

The restoration of the car's body is seldom like changing the location of doors, windows, or permanently fixed parts to convert from steel top to make a convertible. It is more like cutting rusted metal to make it disappear. Tom Boutos performed such restoration on B342NZ, but he also did more than corrective welding to protect safety of passengers.

The next steps required the most time of all. The car's balance is at stake, and how the spaces between panels are painstakingly made equal. Balancing the body on the chassis, removing and adjusting it several times were required. Fitting of the bonnet to the cowl and fenders, making sure the doors close properly, and the window regulators function properly are all included with this responsibility. If not, the metal fabricator's work may have to be modified; in many respects nothing is done until perfection is achieved. A casual visitor to the body and paint shop might think good enough was enough, but when two sets of artists work for two and a half years, perfection is not only desired, but expected.

B342NZ being inspected by an RREC Member

The result expected is merely to reproduce the car to its original grandeur, from a product that might not justify that effort except for a rare car as Sir John's Bentley: his original concept for creating the Bentley that makes the car return to its original culture; Sir John's legacy expressed as a continuing monument after about 50 years after his death, and Stuart Peck's first and only completely designed car in its entirety. A one-off rendition of a Master's touch as his one and only completed art work. And the work of Mulliners of Birmingham, for many years a supplier of bodies to Standard Motors, of which Sir John served as Managing Director for over 20 years. And, this being the first and last post-war luxury car with Bentley (and Rolls Royce) typifying the power and glamour built by these individuals and firms.

The team of craftsmen worked for four years to achieve the product of the original skilled workmen who required two years to create Sir John's car in the first place are pleased to have restored this rare vehicle for the public's enjoyment and in honor of:

- Sir John Black's service to his country and to sports-car enthusiasts,
- To the achievement of Stuart Peck, the designer who cleverly integrated English and French design into the car, and
- Mulliners of Birmingham for its hand-manufacture of B342NZ.

People's objectives for selecting a color or a combination of colors often varies in their desire to achieve specific results.

We lack knowledge about Sir John's purposes, but his decision overruled the color recommended by his designer Stuart Peck who wanted a black body with blue combination. Sir John selected a black color only. Obviously their preferences differed.

To avoid such a problem, I have worked with a paint-color consultant in California, Roy Dryer, on this opportunity to vary our choices. We agree on an objective or set of them, to make the choices consistent.

In the matter with the '52 Bentley, we carefully studied the circumstances we wished to emphasize, or to avoid. With the Bentley we like certain features in both categories.

To gain favorable sighting we wished to gain an image of low to the road, setting length, smooth speed in motion, fast in speed, and in support. We painted 120 combinations of sketches and tacked them on an outside wall for viewing. We made choices on the least desirable, towards the most desirable, removing the least preferable.

A look at a photograph of the car in this process, provides most viewers support for these results. Then we faced the most desirable on metal. We apparently made the best combination of colors on the B342NZ.

Our objective was to leave an impressive image of speed, sleekness in appearance, both with colors and contours of curves and harmony, all with a blending of shades and shadows that reflect speeds instead of movement through steel objects. A box car figure does not achieve a figure as our Mark VI Bentley. Evidence related by people indicates we achieved the objectives.

Yes, much the same may be achieved with opposites of blends by shocking the senses of color shades too. The curves did not leave us with that impact nor did our senses make us feel cool and warm to the same effect. Sir John's Car Is Restored and Preserved

The top extenuates the bodyline curves

I thought this day would never be reached. There comes a day when enough is enough, and that day had been reached, almost.

Even professionals have different opinions on when a restoration is completed. Those working as metal fabricators come closest to knowing when their work is done; that is when all bad wood and metal has been replaced, when structural integrity is restored, and conformation is achieved, with proper gaps and margins in place. Theirs is an engineering function, a call of metal physics, organic metallurgical chemistry, and the science and art of metal design and shaping.

B342NZ went through that phase for 13 months of effort by one professional, devoting 6.5 days each week, to the end when the car was his, and he was the car. Such devotion is seldom purchased with money. Tom Boutos and I spent many hours in conversation envisioning the ideology of Sir John to clarify his vision of this car, whose purpose he never made known but perhaps to a few of his subordinates. It never made it into print.

Tom would explain the work of each of the metal fabricators as the car was being built at Mulliners of Birmingham, and explain what was done by master metal workers, and what was done by apprentices. He would expound on the repairs made during the years the car was raced, by the differences in the type of repairs made. He was as an archeologist in trying to understand an earlier period. That is the work of a metal fabricator like Tom when he works on a rare car. His work was different in many important ways from that of others involved with B342NZ.

About a month after its schedule at Pebble Beach, the car was shown at Ironstone Concours d'Elegance, located in Murphys, California, a picturesque entrance to the Sierra Nevada Mountains. I have shown cars at Ironstone on many occasions, but not for about 8 years because I had no car worthy of showing. This year there were 460 cars on exhibit, a worthy field for B342NZ. The car was judged "Best of Class and later in the afternoon, "MOST ELEGANT OPEN CAR". We were pleased.

The following week we showed the Bentley at the Niello Concours at Serrano, a 30 miles distance east of Sacramento, in the sun belt of the Sacramento Valley. There, from among 260 cars on display, she again was judged "Best of Class", and then "BEST OF SHOW". Needless to say, we were ecstatic, again. "The preserved version of Sir John's Bentley was reached."

Final colors of B342NZ

CHAPTER 9

The "Laws" of Statistical Chance

We believe John Black accomplished great results in the management of Standard Motors. He also engaged in a career with public service that embraced serving national public matters. Some of these involved two world wars as an officer of several military units. During this service he was severally injured, but at those moments, he managed industrial industries where he built war materials, trucks, airplanes, and battle winning events that were very successful.

As reported, King George VI recognized him as a national figure, culminating in a knighthood and the title of Sir John Black. Any person with such public service accomplishments as he had performed as an industrialist with these rare achievements is worthy of such honor, known as Sir John Black. Few citizens are so well honored.

"Well done", Sir John. You are truly properly honored by the Royal Government for tremendous achievements, and several of which may be at industrial levels and deserving greater industrial recognition than currently bestowed.

Then too, his accomplishments in the automobile sector were also creative, and his achievements were awesome as an unusual supplier of major car components to his competitors. Apparently, those were also successful to Standard Motors.

At least fourteen car competitors became substantial direct competitors of his, without which components they would be unable to survive. Truly, he enabled the British recreational and sports car post-war industry to develop into a major international competitor in most of the regions of this great growth. That was also a wise business decision for Standard Motors to develop its own growth plans.

I have not known William Lyons, the developer of the Jaguar, but I suspect he and John might have been interesting rascals and true competitors.

I didn't have any knowledge of John Black either, or any of his family, but life must have had strong bloodlines of what I have heard. His personal life was like a career for some people, but John seemingly crammed several lifetimes into his.

We are unfamiliar with what we now mention, but being what seems to be consistent of what I think of John, he must have been very well supplied with associates who helped him achieve some of it all. I suggest the reader of this document pick up the book titled Triumph and Tragedy, by Nick Black, for more information about Sir John's co-workers.

Under the bonnet of B342NZ

Stuart Peck – a wonderworker

Often there is a member of a project who outshines others. In the case of this Bentley it was Stuart Peck, a man of moderate achievement in earlier days. He had a modest reputation for working with small sports car designers, for limited years in car design.

His reputation may not have been outstanding, but that may have been a negative evaluation by a corps of rivals. Yes, he worked on project cars with other designers as an assistant, but that was his pride to learn skills. He was successful in creating his own styles. To evaluate his work with that of others, one needs to compare their cars and you will often find Peck's work creative in contrast.

Years after his completed work on Sir John's Bentley, he traveled to California to observe works being produced there, including cars shown at Pebble Beach. His was a declining skill because of the development of factory-made cars with all of their benefits.

In the craft of auto design, it is the composite of decisions that controls all the pride or disappointments of the item being manufactured.

We often start our restoration activity with artwork using pen and ink, or chalk sketching, followed by contours, followed by paints. On Sir John's car we made about 120 paint combinations that we placed on walls to observe which basic color combinations achieved the desired results. Some didn't survive the wall evaluations, and those were discarded. The final evaluations were the result of such paint schemes, and the compensation is keen. We do not know how Stuart made these choices, but the magnitude of our numbers is huge and exciting and changes with sunlight or overcast light conditions.

The responsibility is more difficult when only one car is involved in a restoration because one has fewer options for choice. Also, a designer must have memories tucked in his memory from what curves, for example, may look best with what color and curvature. It is a difficult, thankless responsibility except when the result is as beautiful as on this Bentley.

When the result is expensive or the conditions are difficult, we may fabricate a partial metal mock-up to have a real pattern.

Stuart made decisions that reflected excellent judgments by using French designs that resulted in perfect results even on English bodies.

It would seem that Stuart Peck deserved more acknowledgement than he was frequently given in reviews.

In retrospect, the credit for finding this rare car is on balance. There is ample credit for the finding and the description of the decision to build the car by Sir John Black.

The decision of Stuart Peck follows more judiciously. If that was a wise decision, retaining Stuart Peck seems a very wise decision by Sir John Black.

Having a decision that resulted in this car was prudent, but with little interest or emotion at the time, shows a breakdown in its fiber. If it were not for the decisions of *Kurt and Molly Hammerstrom,* the car's existence would be unknown. After 28 years in storage by the Hammerstroms, even the concept of such a car would not be significant because of the theoretical knowledge of its existence and the success of the factory's taking over the Mark VI model. The memory of obsolescent projects over time may have evaporated.

That brings up a "so-what" from such a legend. The car could be a legend and perhaps a dream, or sold as a parts car with no interest to add value to the concept.

Let's "assume" one more circumstance. Suppose we bring forth it's " basket case existence", but with limited reality for restoration? Suppose no one came forth for the desired value of the car, even when it was brought forward. Can you imagine its validity for value? The probability of a low value is quite significant, with no favorable interest. Obviously the "Science" of Statistical Chance can exist, and its value for restoration disappear.

Many outcomes are measured in terms of the chance a course of action may have of happening. In the matter of this Bentley, the following events happened that suggest whether the "science of chance" had a part in the outcome or whether it was a "good" chance?

Outcome 1. The decision of Sir Black needing a Prototype car to establish a successful line of sports cars?

The chance of such car life after succeeding and the chance of surviving a long life in England?

The chance that a Californian would buy the car and continue its life was not an option when Kurt Hammerstrom succumbed.

After surviving two owners, there was only one potential buyer who could maintain the survival of the car.

Result:

Could these unlikely results really be combined so that the car is now available for generations?

Obviously "That Outcome Has Been Assured" by the car's completion.

Dr Kurt and Molly Hammerstrom placed the dismantled car in storage, assuming the global population of sports car enthusiasts, especially for Bentleys, would attempt a rescue. Society is now assured of a permanent survivalist into the future for generations. A fat chance? It has happened.

The Final Mystery from Conception to Survival Preservation

It's a story worth the admiration of sports car enthusiasts and Bentley devotees.

Kurt and Molly Hammerstrom are key members of the group of prior owners of the Bentley whose contributions are as vital as that of John Black and Stuart Peck. They were second from last owners of the Bentley without whose involvement for nearly 30 years enabled the continuation of the entire course of owners.

Their intent was to restore the car after they found it a pleasure to drive, yet they realized it required a complete restoration. That led them to place the car in dry storage, and to dismantle the car into containers well marked. Kurt never survived the intentions, and eventually Molly continued with the storage. She likely considered selling it as a parts car, but found that a difficult decision in respect for Kurt's memories. For many years it remained in storage until her fateful decision, that the car be sold as a restoration car project. Had that decision not been made, neither John Black nor Stuart Peck would likely be remembered for their original accomplishments because there was no other buyer at the time of the sale in 2010. Kurt and Molly should be commended for their decisions as well as John Black and Stuart Peck for theirs, who at the time were both deceased.

But, there's still one more feature to the story needed to complete the mysteries of possibly the rarest Bentley Mark VI ever manufactured. It's a story that created the beginning of the B342NZ, the end of its restoration and, likely, its survival. The last, of which, is properly credited to Dr. Leon Garoyan of Davis, California, who owned the car for 10 years. During his ownership, Garoyan solely funded and oversaw the complete restoration and held the title until it was sold at auction at Monterey, California as a completely restored car. Had he not desired to restore the car for posterity, there would be no story.

During the restoration process, Garoyan brought together his amazing team of technicians to collaborate on full restoration and preservation taking six years to locate or fabricate the parts needed to fully rebuild the car to its glory and reintroduce it to the world's auto enthusiasts.

During Garoyan's ownership, the B342NZ began its prize-winning, show-car life, earning a "Best of Show" and "Most Elegant Open Car" while in his possession, all with the tank full of gasoline needed to prove it is without peer, carrying its award winning legacy into perpetuity. It now starts a new story.

The track from conception to final restoration and survival of the Bentley B342NZ has been a historically interesting path that illustrates "concept of statistical chance work".

Each part has been a necessary, randomized, significant past events, with a partially consumable and destructive phase.

Those in the preservative construction group consist of Sir John Black, who conceived the concept and paid for its *original* construction. Leon Garoyan, owner, restorer, and editor and Chris Clarke, President, J & N Classic, Inc. All parts and sales charges were paid by Garoyan for the public's enjoyment.

The car entered my life (and therefore, Nina's also) in October 2010, and during the ensuring nearly eight years it maintained five families within 100 miles of Davis, with most within 25 miles. Many friends who are receiving this message contributed to the achievement of collecting a mass of parts, requests for assistance, information, some hand holding and guidance. The end product is a miracle of bringing to life a vision of one person, Sir John Black, who envisioned a result that no one I know has been able to explain. We know some features of the car's design appear on the TR3, a sports car still a collector's item. Some believe the car was a prototype for the Triumph sports car. I enjoyed and benefited from having contacts with Nick Black, Sir John's youngest son. He was very helpful as we proceeded with our efforts that led to a preservation of a one-off creation.

The car is gone from my presence, but many of us will remember it and what it has meant to us, and many of our friends who have contributed to this car. It is gratifying that now the car has returned to its original grandeur. It was not always roses and wine, but for me, it has been an achievement I have experienced with but a few of the lovely cars my friends and I have restored together.

We, my family and our friends, can hope that the next owner of the car will contribute to making Sir John a continuing memorial to an English industrialist whom King George VI honored for his contributions to his country and for mankind. I would have been proud to have known him.

Leon Garoyan's Restoration Team from Start Through Completion were:

Tom Boutos, Sacramento, Ca. Steel Craftsman, Wood Trim (deceased)

Roy Dryer, Chicago Park, Ca. Paint Designs, Artist

Richard Biner, Carmichael, Ca. Upholsterer, Trimming

Jerry's (Lucky) Paints, Sacramento, Ca. Paint Blends

Jeff Norene, (Lee's Vintage), West Sacramento, Ca. Paint Application

Steven Bennet, West Sacramento, Ca. Paint Application

Steven Galdrige, Carmichael, Ca. Machine Mechanic

Mark Milton, Woodland, Ca. Mechanic

Jerry Nishimoto, Davis, Ca. Information Technology Support